Where was this book when I was becoming a teacher? It is wise, fun, practical, and memorable. If I were redesigning teacher preparation and development, this book would be front and center. Brilliant job! Buy the book and keep it close by.

—**Dr. Fred Mednick,** founder, Teachers Without Borders

Jake's [inclusion of] McKinsey and Company research clearly outlines the skills, knowledge, and attributes students will need to be prepared for their future, not our past, in a workplace transformed by AI and other advancing technologies.

—**Dr. Bill Daggett,** founder and chairman, International Center for Leadership in Education

This book is a roadmap to creating effective, engaging, and equitable classrooms. Aligned with Universal Design for Learning (UDL), it offers versatile strategies to enhance students' critical thinking, collaboration, and digital fluency. A must-have for teachers who aspire to teach better, work less!

—**Dr. Donya Ball,** author, *Against the Wind: Leadership at 36,000 Feet*

This book equips ELA educators with the essential tools to teach students to think for themselves. It offers questioning strategies, public speaking skills, and collaboration methods that empower students to become independent and critical thinkers.

—**Nathan Collins,** English teacher and edTech consultant

EduProtocols are wonderful tools, not only in the US but globally. Jacob Carr's ELA teaching ideas are fantastic, and I can't wait to use them. Incorporating generative AI into the mix makes it even more relevant for modern classrooms.

—**Gábor Kertész,** junior high school teacher, Canton Zürich, Switzerland

Jacob Carr's EduProtocols are adaptable to any content area and grade level. This guidebook empowers students while giving teachers strategies to build classroom communities. It engages students successfully and allows teachers to enjoy life outside school.

—**Maria Gallagher,** fourth-grade teacher, Roxbury School District, NJ

Jacob Carr equips educators with powerful tools to engage students in meaningful literary exploration and critical thinking. Whether you're seasoned or new, this book will inspire you to create an environment where every student can thrive.

—**Josephine Wozniak,** middle school teacher

The *EduProtocol Field Guide ELA Edition* is an invaluable tool for both new and experienced teachers. If you are interested in the synergy of creativity and efficiency in facilitating student-centered learning, this guide will help you dive right in with your students tomorrow! The teaching frames are adaptable and reproducible, which allows teachers to put more energy and creativity into their content.

—**Kristin Lower,** English teacher

The latest EduProtocols book is a game-changer for ELA classrooms. Jacob Carr's innovative activities and clear guidance will help teachers bring literature to life.

—**Alan Alcala,** middle school teacher

This book is loaded with new EduProtocols that will transform any classroom. It's a great resource for any subject. As a social studies teacher, I see its value across all content areas.

—**Drew Skeeler,** sixth-grade social studies teacher, Barwise Middle School

Jake's EduProtocols are accessible and easy to execute across all content areas. This book supports those looking to lift EduProtocols, fostering students' growth in content knowledge, skills, and mindset. It's a transformative tool for educators.

—**Ariana Hernandez,** science teacher and author of *EduProtocols Science Field Guide*

This book makes me want to teach full-time, and I'm starting year thirty! The pedagogy is K-12, and I appreciate Jake's candid narrative. I'm excited for new ways to engage learners and try the new EduProtocols with my K-5 students.

—**Kim Voge,** educator and consultant, author, *Deploying EduProtocols*

Jake Carr's book is like having a supportive coach. His student-centered protocols empower students to embrace challenges confidently, making it a must-read for educators looking to enrich their classroom practices.

—**Justin Unruh,** high school teacher

Jake's strategies enhance student engagement across disciplines. His inclusive methods simplify workloads while creating dynamic, interactive learning environments, making teaching a joy with less stress.

—**Alfredo Silva,** social studies department chair

Few educators bring as much ingenuity and foresight into the classroom as Jacob Carr. Fewer still are teachers who do so with as much personality, grace, and forethought to facilitate space for students to boldly retake their education on themselves. Jake's work is a novel guidepost in the seismic present and still settling future of education.

—**Scott Bootman,** English and philosophy educator, CORE Butte High School/ Butte College

I couldn't put this book down! Jake's passion and personal challenges are woven into every chapter. I'm excited to introduce ELA EduProtocols into my science classes, blending academic rigor with social growth.

—**Christine Miramontes,** science teacher and author, *EduProtocols Science Field Guide*

The EduProtocol Field Guide ELA Edition is a game-changer. Jacob Carr's innovative EduProtocols have revolutionized my teaching approach, creating a dynamic learning environment. This book is a must-have for any educator.

—**Lisa Moe,** sixth-grade teacher

Jacob Carr's book is a game-changer for ELA classrooms. His innovative EduProtocols are easy to implement and instantly impactful. With these new frameworks, learning becomes engaging and dynamic. Remember, "Go slow to go fast!"

—**Shawn Reed,** sixth-grade teacher

Mr. Carr's passion for teaching shines in the ELA edition of EduProtocols. His innovative use of EduProtocols exemplifies the motto "Teach better, work less." This edition features new, tested protocols alongside fresh takes on familiar ones. A must-read for all teachers, it promotes student ownership of learning and 21st-century skills.

—**Dr. Valerie Sun,** principal and dual language advocate

The EduProtocol Field Guide ELA Edition

Bring Your Teaching into Focus

THE EduProtocol FIELD GUIDE
ELA EDITION

— 10 —

Student-Centered Lesson Frames for Deepening Student Involvement

Jacob Carr

with Jon Corippo & Marlena Hebern

The EduProtocol Field Guide ELA Edition: 10 Student-Centered Lesson Frames for Deepening Student Involvement

© 2024 Jacob Carr with Jon Corippo and Marlena Hebern

This book is available at special discounts when purchased in quantity for educational purposes or for use as premiums, promotions, or fundraisers. For inquiries and details, contact the publisher at books@daveburgessconsulting.com.

Published by Dave Burgess Consulting, Inc.

San Diego, CA

DaveBurgessConsulting.com

Library of Congress Control Number: 2024941449

Paperback ISBN: 978-1-956306-83-5

Ebook ISBN: 978-1-956306-84-2

Cover and interior design by Liz Schreiter

Edited and produced by Reading List Editorial

ReadingListEditorial.com

This book is dedicated to the transformative power of the EduProtocols community, a beacon of curiosity and passion in my teaching journey. My heartfelt gratitude to Jon and Marlena for inviting me into this revolutionary endeavor. To Wonder Goddess of the Universe, also known as my wife, Julie, my unwavering support and guiding star, thank you for believing in me and helping me in immeasurable ways. To my family, your understanding and pride in my work has been my solace and strength during my absences. And to the myriad of educators and students I've encountered along the way, your passion fuels my commitment. Together, we weave a tapestry of learning enriched by gratitude and shared knowledge.

Contents

Foreword

Bored, bored, bored.

Bored *and* frustrated.

I was sitting in my junior English class in high school when I started to consider becoming a teacher.

I wish I could tell you that it was inspired, engaging instruction that sparked a passion for teaching in me. Unfortunately, it was quite the opposite.

My English teacher was very, very traditional. She knew the chapters of her textbook as if they were tattooed on the inside of her forearm. (Come to think of it, she did wear long sleeves a lot. Maybe they *were* tattooed on her forearm.)

She had a worksheet for everything. And if we didn't do the worksheets, we were probably answering the questions in the textbook at the end of the lesson.

Did literature and prose come to life for me in that classroom? Nope. Not even close.

So, to combat my boredom and frustration in that class, high school junior Matt started playing a game. It was the "How Would I Teach This Differently?" game. (Did you ever play this as a student?)

After school, I would go home and vent my frustration to my mom. "It's so boring! If she would only do this and this and this, English class would be so much more interesting."

Oh, what I would have given to have an English teacher like Jacob Carr.

In this book you're holding now, Jacob shares a new vision for teaching English. It's a vision where students feel empowered, where they're met with challenges that are right on their level. It's a vision that leads to less teacher burnout through the mantra "Teach better, work less."

It's a vision packed full of EduProtocols, lesson frames with *your* curriculum that students actually look forward to—and that can drive real academic results.

In this book, you'll get a vivid description of this vision and a road map to realize it in your classroom.

Years later, I went back to college to study education and ended up teaching high school Spanish (and after that, I began teaching teachers through my work at Ditch That Textbook).

My frustration as a student led me to become a teacher. Unfortunately, that path isn't common for most students. They usually just tune us out—and some of them channel their frustration into classroom disruptions and attention-seeking behavior.

Oh, what I would have given to have an English teacher like Jacob Carr.

I have good news, though.

You can *be* an English teacher like Jacob Carr.

This book takes you right into his classroom. He shares practical examples that worked for his students—and that helped him get out the classroom door at a reasonable hour to live his life.

And, as any good English-teacher-turned-author does, Jacob draws you in with his wit and crafty storytelling.

English teachers: Read this book. Then use it as a reference guide, flipping back to your favorite protocols to add them to your lesson plans.

Your students will thank you. And then you'll thank Jacob as you step out the doors of the school to get back to living your life.

—Matt Miller, author, speaker, educator, and creator of Ditch That Textbook

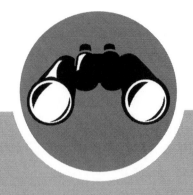

SECTION 1

Let's Get Started

Introduction

I used to feel like a lousy teacher-parent. You know, the one who works hard at their own kid's school and finds their child asleep in the back of the classroom at 5:00 p.m. The one who grades papers on the sidelines of soccer practice, works on the couch during bedtime routines, and goes to work on Sundays. They're good teachers, but they're also burning out. I used to be one of those teachers, but I devised a plan instead of letting burnout drive me from my career.

Step 1 was to leave an environment that required an unreasonable workload. Step 2 was to wrangle my processes and "Teach better, work less." That wrangling began with the Edu-Protocols. I went from an exhausting, unhealthy relationship with work to enjoying what I do, innovating my pedagogy, and relishing my time with students once more. I went from sending out non-teaching job inquiries to loving my career again.

So, when did my relationship to my job change?

In the late summer of 2018, I started at a new school where I looked forward to teaching a fresh subject. I had spent the decade prior as an elementary and middle school teacher. In my new position, I was finally getting to teach English at the high school level, which was my plan. So, I transitioned from teaching spelling, arithmetic, and handwriting to third graders and began teaching English to a combination of freshmen and sophomores. It was exhilarating, and it was terrifying.

I imagine the fear my principal read on my face those first few weeks as I entered the waters. Would I be able to under-

I wanted to share this picture of "tired Jake." It was real. I loved teaching at that time, but it wasn't sustainable. Just look at those tired eyes!

stand these older students quickly enough? Would I be able to adapt to a new subject and staff? "I heard something about a new book," he said one day, stopping by my desk. "It could be interesting." So, after a few moments of searching the web, I could see change coming; I purchased *The EduProtocol Field Guide: Book 1,* on August 30, 2018. It was in my hands a few days later, and I was ready to dive in.

My classes soon began working on our first EduProtocol, a Group Brainstorm, wrapping our heads around the setting of a novel. We dove into a Worst Preso Ever and an Iron Chef Lesson, looking at the main characters a little later. When we tried our first round of Fast and Curious, the laughter-filled moans of defeat, the cheering, and the cheesy background music bled into the hallway, causing the principal to peek in. He stayed, and he played. The EduProtocols were working. No, they were working well.

So many days began with me saying, "OK, everyone. I've got a new EduProtocol for you. We might hate it, and we might not." I called it *guinea pigging,* and students loved it. They knew they could help steer what we did. Every time we did something new, students gave me feedback on what worked and didn't. I threw a slew of EduProtocols at them: Cyber Sandwich, Iron Chef Lesson, Fast and Curious, 8 p*ARTS, Thin Slides, and more. I packed that novel study unit so full of EduProtocols that I knew we would create magic or a terrible storm.

It was pure magic.

Kids engaged, laughed, presented other students' work without preparation (thanks, Worst Preso!), and crawled deep into the novel's themes. By the time they were writing their final essays on the book, they felt like they were getting away with cheating. It was awesome. That year, I even had a single-language French speaker and a deaf English/Spanish learner in the same class! This (along with all the typical needs of a classroom) was eased by this new project. Some kids began attending my class for fun during their free periods even though they weren't enrolled. They were all in, and they were all getting what they needed.

Then our world changed. On the morning of November 8, 2018, the Camp Fire ravaged and destroyed the areas around Paradise, California, a mountain community where some of the students lived. Many of our students and staff became homeless within hours, and a new sense of trauma flowed into the county.

In the fire, my whole childhood burned down. The school where I played the giant in a kindergarten play. The small cinema where I had my first date. The late-night diner where my friends and I would hang out after football games, and so much more. The only home my parents had known, two aunts' homes, my brother's house, and so many more sentimental places succumbed to one of California's deadliest and most destructive wildfires. In hours, it destroyed 95 percent of the structures in the area and claimed the lives of at least eighty-five individuals. My students' community and sense of safety vaporized that day.

County schools stayed closed until after Thanksgiving break. When we finally returned, we were devastated but glad to see each other. With evacuation orders in effect until early December, students and staff lived in RVs and hotels or on family members' couches. Some lived in a makeshift tent city in the Walmart parking lot. Some of them showed up the first day worried that they had no supplies and that their books

Kelly and Phyllis Carr (Jake's parents) standing before the remains of their home in Paradise, CA, after the fire.

had burned. We even shared our campus with a middle school needing a safe place to operate. After living in a smoky, apocalyptic haze for so many weeks, we began to accept that the homes of one-third of our students, and many of our staff members, were lost.

But what does this all have to do with EduProtocols? Over a few years, floods, power outages, wildfires, a dam failure, and even a global pandemic disrupted the educational experience in my county many times. Yet throughout these challenges, the one thing that helped students continue their learning was familiarity and routine. EduProtocols held their trembling hands.

When COVID-19 stay-at-home orders began in March 2020, a student with clinical anxiety emailed me. He was worried about how school was going to happen. He wrote, "Hi, Mr. Carr. My mom says we aren't going back to school Monday. You'll probably give us some EduProtocols to work on, and we'll probably write some slides. If that changes, let me know." He felt empowered. He knew what to expect and even how to do it. With the EduProtocols the students had already practiced, I cobbled together quick journaling activities and pushed those assignments out through Google Classroom. They were nothing fancy, but they were suitable, predictable actions to advance students' learning in the face of uncertainty.

But we don't live in a constant state of disruption. EduProtocols don't only work when students face a catastrophe. Sure, my deep respect for EduProtocols came from the difficulty my community experienced. Not only did the students continue learning and feeling a sense of togetherness through hard times, but they also retained a little piece of their world, something consistent and predictable. But my absolute love of EduProtocols comes from peaceful times, like the laughter I hear during Game of Quotes and the best Worst Preso moments. The most important thing to understand is that through EduProtocols, kids who don't like English or struggle with the material can succeed just as well as the advanced kids. This is because of the consistency, predictability, accessibility, and culture that the EduProtocols help build.

You are somewhere on the spectrum of workload. Are you at the deep, despairing end like I was in the beginning? Or are you closer to teaching bliss? Wherever you are, implementing some EduProtocols will make things better. For example, once I started using EduProtocols, I found that my planning time, grading time, and general workload decreased significantly. At the same time, student performance increased, students' stress around the subject diminished, and frankly, everyone was happier.

What's my workload like now? I leave my bag at work most days. When I do take it home, it usually stays closed. I get time with my family and friends. I don't feel controlled by an oppressive career, and my students are progressing and are happy. And not only are my students achieving and learning more, but they're having fun!

So, dive in. Maybe you've used EduProtocols already; perhaps they're all brand new. Either way, dip a toe in the water and try new things.

I hope that every English Language Arts teacher finds invaluable tools here. If you're at the Advanced Placement (AP) level, the EduProtocols in this book will specifically help you make content more accessible to your students. In these chapters, you'll find AP-specific adaptations and correlations to the Enduring Understandings. You'll also find the tools your students need in order to read, analyze, generalize, discuss, and argue the facets of rhetorical construction. Tools for more profoundly understanding fiction analysis and crosscutting thematic information are here, too.

However, if you're not in the AP/College Board world, don't worry; EduProtocols are easily permutable down through the middle grades. Many teachers use these EduProtocols across all grades and subjects (check out Repuzzler for one great example of an adaptable activity).

Implementing EduProtocols is a practice of discovery. Find out what you and your students like and what you hate. But most importantly, with EduProtocols you should feel confident that your students are learning the required curriculum and everyone is healthy, happy, and having a great time in the process.

What Are EduProtocols?

EduProtocols are lesson frames into which you will insert your curriculum to teach more effectively and deliver more engaging content. By incorporating these lesson frames, you can streamline lesson planning, grading, and much more. The net effect of implementing EduProtocols, even if it's just a few to start out with, is increased engagement, decreased stress for students and teachers alike, and an overall positive culture shift in the classroom.

Each EduProtocol embodies some form of the Four Cs (although there are a few exceptions, like Fast and Curious). The Four Cs, identified by the Partnership for 21st Century Skills, are four skills considered essential for modern students, skills that successful adults use every day in and out of the workplace:

> **Jake**
> A teacher who recently attended one of my online workshops said this as a reflection: "The introduction of EduProtocols across our school has ushered in a paradigm shift in teaching methodologies and student outcomes."

- **Collaboration:** Using interpersonal and intrapersonal skills when working with peers.
- **Communication:** Sharing one's work, research, and projects with other students and adults inside and outside the four walls of the classroom.
- **Critical Thinking:** Analyzing problems, data, research, literature, or mathematics by solving real-world problems.
- **Creativity:** Open-ended and choice-driven activities in which students have autonomy in the process and results so creativity can flourish.

You can find detailed information about the Four Cs in chapter 14, "The Four Cs Throwdown," in *The EduProtocol Field Guide: Book 1*. The important thing is that as teachers, we want to see our students collaborating, creating, critically thinking, and communicating, and we want you to know that you can use the ideas presented here to enrich student engagement through the Four Cs and change your classroom!

By their very nature, EduProtocol lesson frames are adaptive as the curriculum changes and students move from one topic to another in their studies. Once teachers have learned a particular lesson frame, they are able to repeat that lesson frame again and again with a variety of content throughout the year. This allows students to gain familiarity with a process that can be used repeatedly for learning. It's amazing how willing and able students are to work through difficult material when they don't have to simultaneously figure out *how* to work through it. This is one of the best parts of EduProtocols implementation: students know how to do what you're asking them, so they get to focus on the material itself.

EduProtocols are suitable for students across the grade span from kindergarten through adult learners, and they allow the learner to engage with the Four Cs (collaboration, communication, critical thinking, and creativity) in a format that works with Universal Design for Learning (UDL). This helps remove barriers to student learning and increase access to the content. Not all of the protocols tap into all of the Four C skills, but most do at varying levels.

EduProtocols are also accessible for educators. So, even as EduProtocols challenge students to dig deeper, they keep the teaching technology fairly straightforward: most protocols use Google Slides or PowerPoint as their foundation.

Managing Cognitive Load with EduProtocols

EduProtocols are effective because they were designed with students' cognitive needs in mind. When students jump from one activity to the next, day after day, they can lose their ability to focus on content. Perpetually learning and relearning tasks causes wear and tear for students. EduProtocols allow students to learn one task and then apply it to a variety of content lessons, thus maximizing their energy and focusing their effort on the content at hand.

You may have heard of the sweet spot for learning, called the zone of proximal development (ZPD), a concept developed by Lev Vygotsky in the 1930s. ZPD describes a state of mind when a learner is working in the space between "cannot complete on my own" (frustration) and "can completely do on my own" (boredom). When students work in the space between *cannot* and *can*, they are challenged at just the right level and are most open to new learning. Too much, too fast, and the learner shuts down. Too little, too slow, and the learner does not pay close attention because they already know it all. When it's just right, the learner excels. For further discussion of this, check out the Lifting EduProtocols in chapter 21.

Because EduProtocols manage cognitive load, they build optimal ZPD into the student experience. This is the magic dust of the EduProtocols that makes all their other goodness possible. By scaffolding learning with the EduProtocols, we allow our students to become hyperfocused on course content instead of lesson design. Students, regardless of age, feel enormously successful when they accomplish a lesson with little direction because they already know how.

If you are trying to wrap your brain around this concept, it's helpful to think of an EduProtocol as the process of posting an image on social media. There are several specific steps to sharing an image on a platform like Instagram:

- Find the perfect shot.
- Snap the image.
- Open the app.
- Add the image to the app.
- Adjust the color and other edit options.
- Write and tag your post with hashtags.
- Wait for your friends to see your picture and comment.

The next time you find that perfect shot, you will repeat the same basic steps to post the image. Those steps remain the same, but the image and the circumstances for taking the perfect shot change each time you post.

Posting a photo feels complicated at first. It's a struggle to find just the right edits. However, with a little practice, the process becomes familiar, and you soon find that your concentration shifts to the art of framing the perfect shot with just the right lighting *instead* of finding the photo library in the app. When finding someone to follow on Instagram, notice how their skill as a photographer has evolved from their earliest posts. Could you imagine how frustrating it would be if the steps to post an image changed with each new photo location?

Could you feel the ZPD shift in the Instagram example? At first, the challenge of Instagram was all about the process of using the application, but later on it became about the artistry of taking a picture.

It takes most classes two to five repetitions of an EduProtocol to master it. The sweet spot is achieved when automaticity is reached, and students' focus shifts from how to complete the process of an EduProtocol to mastering content. When deploying EduProtocols in your classroom, you will feel this shift. Students will recognize the protocol by name and get right to work completing the EduProtocol.

Even the most advanced students stand to gain from the slow implementation of EduProtocols. As students become familiar with a given EduProtocol, they will be able to shift their attention away from the mechanics of lesson procedures and toward the true art and joy of learning. This shift is particularly valuable as students encounter more challenging content at the upper levels of middle school, high school, and AP coursework. Thankfully, the gamified nature of EduProtocols encourages students to take on work that may initially be beyond their comfort zone, further enhancing their learning experience.

The most successful teachers take time in the first weeks of each semester to update students on classroom procedures: where to get paper, when to sharpen pencils, how to put away materials, how to find resources, how to contact the teacher outside of class time, etc. Experienced teachers understand the importance of training and retraining students in the beginning of the year. This early training can give you a head start in deploying protocols with content. But if you're starting late in the year, or you're introducing an EduProtocol midway through the year, simply take time to allow students to learn the process before diving into your content. Go slow to go fast. Your time up front will pay off later.

How to Use This Book

This book provides various effective teaching strategies and tools to enhance your English Language Arts (ELA) instruction at any level. It is written to target the needs of high school educators, but it can be adapted higher or lower depending on your students' familiarity and skill level.

Each chapter focuses on a specific EduProtocol and includes the following sections:

- **Introduction:** This section provides an overview of the EduProtocol and its main objectives.
- **Academic Goals:** This section outlines the specific skills and knowledge that students will develop through the EduProtocol.
- **Teacher Big Ideas:** This section summarizes the key ideas teachers should keep in mind when implementing the EduProtocol.
- **Prepare for the Activity:** This section provides a list of materials and resources you will need to gather before introducing the EduProtocol to your students.

- **Instructions:** This section outlines students' steps to complete the EduProtocol.
- **Key Points to Remember:** This section highlights the most critical takeaways from the EduProtocol.
- **Variations:** This section provides ideas for adapting the EduProtocol to fit the needs and abilities of your students.
- **AP Adaptation and Correlation to the Enduring Understandings:** This section will provide information on how the EduProtocol can be adapted in AP classrooms. It will also include a correlation to the Enduring Understandings, which are the overarching themes and concepts students should take away from the lesson that are testable on the AP Exam.

Whether you are new to teaching ELA or you're an experienced educator, you will find something of value in these chapters. We encourage you to read this book cover to cover to gain a comprehensive understanding of the various EduProtocols available. Alternatively, you can jump from chapter to chapter and pick and choose the tools that best fit your needs and teaching style.

We have included two correlation infographics below to help you decide which EduProtocol might be the most helpful for your class. These infographics provide a quick overview of the skills and objectives that each EduProtocol targets, allowing you to match them to your lesson plans and curriculum easily.

In addition to the main chapters, this book includes two valuable appendices that provide further resources to enhance your teaching practice.

Language & Composition

RHETORICAL SITUATION
- Walk the Line
- #WHASH
- Demosthenor
- YPMG!
- Wicked Hydra
- Unto the Breach
- Repuzzler
- Ikonic
- Iron Chef Lesson
- Group Brainstorm
- Internet Scavenger Hunt
- Research Remixes

CLAIMS & EVIDENCE
- Claim Jumper
- Walk the Line
- AnnoTwist
- Demosthenor
- YPMG!
- Wicked Hydra
- Unto the Breach
- Repuzzler
- Ikonic
- REPP
- Iron Chef Lesson
- Game of Quotes
- Group Brainstorm
- Internet Scavenger Hunt
- Research Remixes

REASONING & ORGANIZATION
- Claim Jumper
- Walk the Line
- AnnoTwist
- Demosthenor
- YPMG!
- Wicked Hydra
- Unto the Breach
- Repuzzler
- Ikonic
- REPP
- Iron Chef Lesson
- Group Brainstorm
- Internet Scavenger Hunt
- Research Remixes

RHETORICAL STYLE
- Claim Jumper
- Walk the Line
- #WHASH
- AnnoTwist
- Demosthenor
- YPMG!
- Wicked Hydra
- Repuzzler
- Ikonic
- REPP
- Iron Chef Lesson
- Group Brainstorm
- Internet Scavenger Hunt
- Research Remixes

Literature

CHARACTER & SETTING
- AnnoTwist
- YPMG!
- Wicked Hydra
- Repuzzler
- Ikonic
- Random Emoji Power Paragraph
- Iron Chef Lesson
- Game of Quotes
- Group Brainstorm
- Internet Scavenger Hunt
- Research Remixes

PLOT, STRUCTURE & SPEAKER
- AnnoTwist
- Demosthenor
- YPMG!
- Wicked Hydra
- Repuzzler
- Ikonic
- Iron Chef Lesson
- Group Brainstorm
- Internet Scavenger Hunt
- Research Remixes

WORD CHOICE, IMAGERY & SYMBOL
- AnnoTwist
- Demosthenor
- YPMG!
- Wicked Hydra
- Unto the Breach
- Repuzzler
- Ikonic
- Random Emoji Power Paragraph
- Iron Chef Lesson
- Game of Quotes
- Group Brainstorm
- Internet Scavenger Hunt
- Research Remixes

COMPARISON
- Walk the Line
- Demosthenor
- YPMG!
- Wicked Hydra
- Repuzzler
- Ikonic
- Iron Chef Lesson
- Group Brainstorm
- Internet Scavenger Hunt
- Research Remixes

ARGUMENT & INTERPRETATION
- Claim Jumper
- Walk the Line
- #WHASH
- AnnoTwist
- Demosthenor
- YPMG!
- Wicked Hydra
- Unto the Breach
- Repuzzler
- Ikonic
- Iron Chef Lesson
- Group Brainstorm
- Internet Scavenger Hunt
- Research Remixes

The first appendix, "UDL Breakdown," details how various EduProtocols align with the principles of Universal Design for Learning (UDL). It covers strategies for engagement, multiple means of action and expression, multiple means of representation, and options for self-reflection and self-regulation. These insights will help you create more inclusive and effective learning experiences for all students.

The second appendix, "Transferrable Skills," aligns EduProtocol activities with essential skills identified by the McKinsey Global Institute's study on future work skills. This appendix highlights how EduProtocols can help students develop critical abilities such as adaptability, critical thinking, collaboration, and digital fluency, ensuring they are well-prepared for the evolving job market.

We hope that you find these ELA EduProtocols to be a valuable resource in your teaching practice. Remember to "Teach better, work less!"

Connect with us on social media:

- @mrcarrontheweb
- @mhebern
- @jcorippo

Visit our website: eduprotocols.com

Jake
Be sure to spend some time on our resource page! Or scan the QR code. You'll find all sorts of student examples, templates, and more on the ever-growing page.

Chapter 1
"But How Do I Start?" Ready, Set, Go!

In the late summer of 2022, I traveled to present at a school in Grand Canyon National Park. After a full day of travel and anticipation, I sadly arrived after sunset and, peering into the abyss, saw only darkness and a few flashes of lightning. However, Peg, my ever-welcoming hostess, told me all about the grandeur of what locals lovingly call "the ditch" and promised that when it came into view, I would see just how amazing it all was.

I slept deeply that night with the sound of rain on the rooftops, dreaming about what I might see come daybreak. Finally, after a strong cup of caffeine and shaking out the nerves I always get before presenting, I ventured to the rim of the canyon on my way to the school. As I crossed the parking lot and came up onto a bit of a rise, the earth dropped out before me; one is never quite prepared to see a landform eighteen miles across and over a mile deep. After my misty eyes cleared (I will always be a nature nerd), I realized something significant about such wonders of the earth: when we first see things that take our breath away and change our perspective of what we know, we don't know where to begin looking.

When teachers are first introduced to the EduProtocols, it can almost feel like looking at the Grand Canyon; we know they're of great value, but we don't know how to begin experiencing them. Thankfully, there are great starting points for implementing Edu-Protocols. I've worked with hundreds of educators, and my suggestion is almost always the same: begin with Thin Slides, Fast and

Jake

Don't forget that your students can be a guide! Watch as they engage with the material. Learn with them. Ask for their opinions and suggestions for bettering your practice. As such, let me introduce Emily to you; you'll see her pop up from time to time in this book, giving a student perspective. Emily took my English class when I was testing out EduProtocols for the first time and is now headed off to college.

Curious, Thin Slide Study Guide, 8 p*ARTS, and Iron Chef Lesson. With those simple "Swiss Army knife" EduProtocols, you can conquer your curriculum for months. I'll treat them briefly here, but for a more in-depth look, check out books 1 and 2 of *The Edu-Protocol Field Guide*.

So, here's a peek under the hood of my classroom and how I start each fresh new group of students. Bite by bite, we eat the elephant and feel nourished.

Jake

You'll see I favor using Google Slides in this book because that's the platform I've used most. But as situations and technologies change, the foundations of these EduProtocols still work; just adjust the platform. And don't diminish how powerful EduProtocols can be on paper, too!

Ready (Thin Slides EduProtocol)

Typically, the first thing I do in my classroom on the first day of class is a Thin Slides EduProtocol. This powerful and ultrasimple EduProtocol sets up an endless supply of skills. Here's how I use it:

1. First, create a shared slide deck with one slide per student.
2. Next, create a title slide with the prompt "What made you smile this summer?"

One word or phrase	One image	One slide	3 minute build time

Using a single slide, students find one picture and/or write one sentence for a word/term that is provided.
Four seconds each to make a claim or observation - The goal is to be done in 5 minutes.

Jake

The templates prevent the endless font selection process and help students create an ultraquick slide. My fastest time is a class of tenth graders doing an informal fallacy Thin Slides EduProtocol in thirty seconds.

Jon

I love how Jake shortens the time once there's clear mastery. We can also add new tasks, such as citing sources, to keep the challenge fresh.

3. Walk students through creating a text box, adding an image, and using the Explore feature in Google Slides. If you use another platform, adjust as you need.

4. Give your students three minutes to add one word describing what made them smile and one picture that shows it, and use the Explore function to apply a simple template for the design.

5. When time is up, revoke editing access and present the deck.

6. Advance slides in the Present mode. When a student's slide pops up, they have about ten seconds to tell the class what made them smile.

Why do I start with Thin Slides? This activity sets a lot of expectations for an EduProtocols Mindset classroom. First, we move fast. We focus on repetition over perfection. With Thin Slides, there's no time for finicky manipulations of pixels, just the right font, the perfect cat meme, etc. This is because often in EduProtocols, it isn't the end product that's important but the mental flip and process.

Second, at least for my setting, Thin Slides is a good starting point because working on the functions of slide creation is essential. Most of what I do is on a slide, and I need students to understand how to build them quickly.

Third, Thin Slides is great because it involves presentation. We present. In my class, we present daily. We do it quickly. We do it without judgment because we're all in the same learning boat.

And fourth, I begin with Thin Slides because it places focus on repetition, not singular products. There are always a few students who don't finish in time, but this crunch is essential to clarify the principle I call the *practice field*.

I often talk about the practice field in our first few days together. I give students a story about a five-year-old who has watched their older siblings play soccer, win trophies, and get a fancy uniform, and it's finally their turn to join the team. I tell them how that little soccer player suits up for the first time, grinning ear to ear, how the coach shows them just how to kick the ball with the inside of their foot instead of the tip of their toe. The little tyke gathers all their glee, runs at the ball, and boots it with the tip of their foot, sending it careening into the street! Cars are screeching to a halt—it's a whole scene. Finally, I tell the students how the coach looks down at their clipboard and, with a wry sense of disapproval, cuts the kid from the team.

Of course, we understand the fundamental flaw of the situation: the child was learning how to kick for the first time and shouldn't have been so harshly judged. But how often do we punish students for learning just like this?

Hence the practice field mentality. I make sure that students know we're practicing. They get credit for the assignment if they're putting in the work and growing. I also ensure they know there's a game for points come Saturday. Practice leads to performance. My duty to them is to create a safe environment to practice new skills. Their duty to themselves is to take advantage of that time so they're prepared for when they have to prove their skills.

Given all these benefits, Thin Slides is also a fast and practical way of replacing entry/exit tickets. It gives me instant feedback on where the class is at. And because the whole class shares through Thin Slides, the EduProtocol provides students a classful of examples for next time.

As you move into using Thin Slides for actual ELA-driven content, here are some prompts I've found useful:

- What is the theme?
- What is the conflict?
- Who is the protagonist?
- What is the central argument?
- What is the weakest claim of the essay?
- Construct an example of parallelism.
- Construct a compound-complex sentence.

Jake

Only you can create a special culture of openness in your classroom. I'm a silly-snarky teacher, and it works well for me. But you do you. Just build a culture that is journey-minded, not endpoint-minded. Process over product!

Set (Fast and Curious EduProtocol)

My next goal at the beginning of the school year is to show students how successful they will become. Thin Slides allows me to demonstrate to students that they're safe with me, but I also need to show them the benefit of playing along with EduProtocols. I do this with Fast and Curious.

Fast and Curious is a gamified way of introducing new information and guiding students in teaching it to themselves. It works with anything that can be formatted as multiple choice and, with a few tweaks, fill in the blank.

One Quick Rep + Immediate Feedback + One More Rep

Watch the class average. Repeat daily!

To introduce Fast and Curious, I create a set of questions using my syllabus and fun facts about me. Then I load those facts up into Gimkit and let the kids play. Not only does this activity teach students what the syllabus contains, but it also gives them space to figure out the platform. And let's talk plainly: this practice also makes sure students know how to navigate the web a little, have their login information, etc. I like giving students a TinyURL or Bitly link to get into the game, which practices something I emphasize a lot in my classroom: the importance of efficiently navigating a web browser. I only play that set once or twice to familiarize students with the content—and more importantly, the process of the EduProtocol. So, what's the process?

Jake

Don't push a web link through an LMS. Students need practice navigating addresses and searching on the internet.

To play Fast and Curious, I use the online platform Gimkit, but Blooket, Wordwall, Quizizz, Quizlet, and anything like that will work; Fast and Curious is a pedagogy, not a platform. Here's how I use it:

1. Search for an existing quiz platform or create one for your use. Just make sure the first time students play, the game isn't content based. They need a few rounds to learn the EduProtocol.

2. Set the game up for a four-minute round.

3. Let students play!

4. Each time a game ends, record the class average.

5. Microteach the top three or four missed concepts.

6. Play another four minutes.

7. Repeat this process daily until a 90 percent to 95 percent correct class average is achieved. This signals that students are ready for a quiz.

Jake

Between rounds of Fast and Curious is a great place to insert Repuzzler, Ikonic, Word-Up Wednesday, Thin Slides, or other ways of microteaching frequently missed concepts.

You will be amazed at just how efficiently students consume material with Fast and Curious. My favorite technique is to have Fast and Curious build students' vocabulary for an upcoming unit. That way, when we start new skills, students have a foundational understanding on which to build.

And don't be afraid to push them with Fast and Curious. I've used 144 Latin and Greek roots all in one set. Really, 144 Latin roots on the first day of class? Sure thing! I don't need my students to know the words instantly; we're building over time. And granted, more complicated concepts with more words will take a few weeks, but with a little done each day and an enjoyable process, students soak up new ideas quickly. For example, after Thanksgiving, I start a set containing twenty-two fallacies and twenty-two

Jake

I like platforms that randomize the questions and continue asking them for a set period instead of asking all the questions only once. At the time of writing, I prefer Gimkit and Blooket for these reasons. Each time students answer incorrectly, it shows them the correct answer, thus incrementally teaching them the information for the next time the question comes around.

Marlena

Building trust is the first step to developing a relationship with your students that will last well beyond the school year.

Jon

Fast and Curious allows us to give AP/CP students 50, 70, or even 100 words per week! I have a message from a teacher who smashed two semesters into one using this technique.

Jake

Hard work gets rewarded! I have a "Box of Unimpressive Prizes" full of stickers, Hi-Chew, dollar-store toys, and other curiosities. I once had a sophomore who was sitting in another class log in and win Fast and Curious in my current period! He came down and collected his prize! I loved every second of it.

biases, and we play that until winter break. Then, when we begin rhetoric in January, students have a solid foundation to start from.

Fast and Curious is great as an ongoing, lower-key EduProtocol. I typically have at least one set of vocabulary for the kids to work on. Perhaps it's a list of difficult words from a reading we're working on or content vocabulary from our unit. I often have a giant GRE or SAT set of terms in Fast and Curious for early finishers to play just for fun. One year during a holiday break, students emailed me to let me know the kit had ended and requested that I set it up again.

Why is this my next go-to EduProtocol? It's fun. It's effective. It's repeatable. It hits the level 1 Depth of Knowledge (DOK) hard, meaning the basic foundational knowledge a student needs and builds on that for expansion. Kids watch their scores as they climb, showing them that they *can* learn.

Go! (Classic EduProtocols Potpourri)

Once I've built a culture where kids feel safe to practice and they have developed digital skills and tasted success by playing along, it's time to dive into course content in a more rigorous way. My three go-to EduProtocols for this are the Thin Slide Study Guide, 8 p*ARTS, and Iron Chef Lesson.

Thin Slide Study Guide EduProtocol

With firm foundations built, students already understand Thin Slides, so it's time to change it up. Thin Slide Study Guide works excellently between rounds of Fast and Curious or even as a stand-alone process. Here's how it works:

Before class, create a shared slide deck with one slide per vocabulary word or concept you're working on. If you need to, double or triple terms to make enough so that each student has one. If there are early finishers, I ask them to complete more than one slide until the deck is complete. Sometimes, I also fill in the incomplete slides as needed.

 + + +  +

One word per student

Google it and define in your own words

One image that describes the term

5 minute build time
4 seconds to share

Key: On Day 2, repeat with another person's slide. On Day 3, repeat with another person's slide.

An example of Thin Slide Study Guide from Jake's 10th-grade English classroom.

Jon

Thin Slide Study Guide is student-made, meaning you get your weekends back. TSSG is graded in real time. You get your weeknights back!

Jake

What about the "they took the slide I wanted" problem? Not a problem! Duplicate it. You get a slide . . . and you get a slide . . . and you get a slide! We are hitting this information multiple ways, so if a term isn't covered because two people did the same one, no worries!

Day 1

1. Each student claims a slide.
2. Students read the existing definition of the vocabulary word and rewrite it in their own words.
3. Students add an image representing the word.
4. Finally, as in Thin Slides, project the deck for the whole class. When a student's slides come up, they tell the class their new definitions. This process should only take a few seconds per slide.

Day 2

1. Direct students to claim a different slide than before.
2. Students rewrite the definition and add it to the slide.
3. Students add another image.
4. Students present to the class. To keep review in mind, I also like to ask the author of the previous day's definition to offer a "thumbs up/down" critique of the new student's revision.

Day 3

1. Repeat the process from Day 2 with each student taking on a new word.
2. Change things up during the presentation portion by having students explain why they chose their picture and how it is the same or different from the previous two days' choices.

Why does Thin Slide Study Guide work, particularly if a student only works on three slides? This EduProtocol is incredibly time and energy efficient. Students hear the entire list of words, definitions, and nonlinguistic representations three times. And don't forget, the information being reviewed is coming in via readings, Fast and Curious, and other modes, too!

*8 p*ARTS EduProtocol*

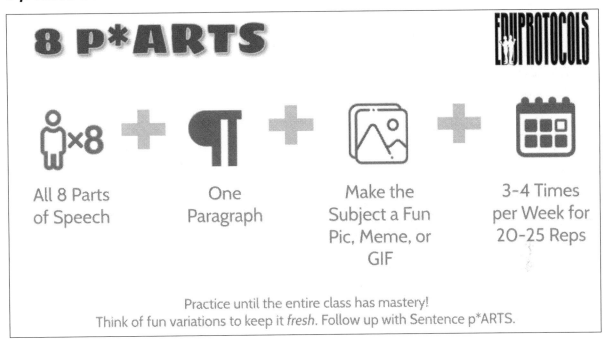

All year, my grammar and mechanics lessons are handled via iterations of the 8 p*ARTS EduProtocol. At its core, 8 p*ARTS is a single sheet that requires students to give examples of the parts of speech and then write them into a paragraph. We typically do a set of these with four to five reps before the material becomes a quiz for points.

Instructions

1. Provide an 8 p*ARTS template. The template has boxes, each labeled with a part of speech (pronoun, verb, article, adjective, adverb, preposition, conjunction, interjection). It also contains a place for students to write a paragraph and a picture or prompt for the students to base their work upon.

2. Choose a picture or text prompt. This can be anything from a painting to a primary source document. The goal is to choose something that will generate interest in the students.

Marlena

All 8 parts of speech in less than four weeks, plus daily creative paragraph writing. Don't review this content; launch the year at full speed.

Jake

Don't forget to snag templates at eduprotocols.com!

3. Have students identify examples of each part of speech in the picture or prompt. They can write their examples in the provided boxes.

4. Once students have filled out the template, have them write a paragraph about the picture or text prompt using all the parts of speech they identified.

5. Last, students share and discuss their paragraphs. This is a great opportunity for students to learn from each other and see how their peers used different word choices to complete their tasks.

8 p*ARTS is effective in that it is a hands-on, engaging way for students to use the parts of speech and solidify their application of them. It also helps students identify vocabulary skills by coming up with new words to use. And it doesn't have to stop there. You can alter the 8 p*ARTS template to ask about different things, such as varied sentence construction, forms of analysis, and many more possibilities. It's a highly valuable and permutable EduProtocol that should be in every teacher's toolkit.

Title		
Your as useful as	A mysterious janitor	Under the football bleachers

Verbs	Adverbs
To make	quickly
To eat	voraciously
To vomit	voluminously

Prepositions
On

Interjections
The horror!

Write a Paragraph using at least ONE of each part of speech

The chef made the food too quickly, and he forgot that the mayonnaise had been in the hot sun all morning. So, when Johnny voraciously ate the tuna salad, he began to vomit voluminously.

The evil Mr. McDonald entered to pick up his class. When he saw the putrid vomit, he shouted, "The horror!" Mr. McDonald demanded that the students clean it up. When they refused, he said, "You are about as useful as the mysterious janitor under the football bleachers!"

Fortunately, Mr. Yost came into the MPR and grabbed the wet mop.

Nouns (one proper)	Adjectives
Vomit	putrid
mop	wet

Conjunctions
and

Pronouns
he

An example of an 8 p*ARTS EduProtocol from Jake's English 10 classroom.

Iron Chef Lesson EduProtocol

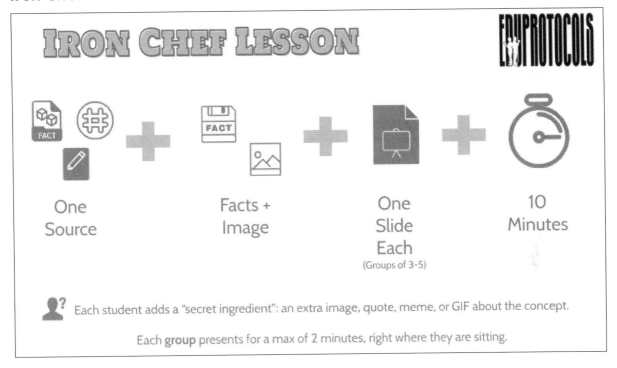

Welcome to the "Swiss Army knife" of EduProtocols. Outside of Fast and Curious and Thin Slides, Iron Chef Lesson is done more than anything else in my classroom. It's a veritable meat-and-potatoes workhorse. A jigsaw at heart, the Iron Chef Lesson is a perfect way of breaking up a text or topics for groups to chew on. Later in this book, you'll see how I've reworked it as Peer Review and Close Reads activities.

Instructions

1. Introduce the Iron Chef Lesson theme and explain the challenge. Each team will be responsible for the slides in a deck, each slide focusing on a specific aspect of the chosen topic.

2. Assign roles within the team. Have the students divide up the work. This will sometimes mean that every student

takes a slide, but it could also result in many different configurations.

3. Provide each student with time and resources to explore their assigned topic (for example, a section of the textbook, text excerpts, images, videos, etc.).

4. Explain the *secret ingredient*. This could be a surprising fact, a thought-provoking question, a multimedia element, or anything that adds a twist to unify each slide within the deck and extend students' knowledge application.

5. Now, set the timer and set them to work.

6. When the timer is up, students will very quickly present their slides to the class.

Iron Chef Lesson gives students a way to not only break down complex topics but also to take ownership of their learning by actively researching, analyzing, and presenting. The flexible structure allows for adaptation to different topics, learning styles, and abilities. It also fosters teamwork and communication as the team works together to complete the task in a way that they devise. Last, the secret ingredient not only fosters creativity and encourages students to think laterally about their topic, but it also works to unify the presentation, creating a common theme.

Marlena

The Iron Chef Lesson is a popular method among teachers for covering classroom content. John Hattie has identified jigsaw activities as having an effect size of 1.20, and summarization activities as having an effect size of 0.79. These strategies can lead to three times the typical year's academic growth for students.

Describe the main plot of Walking Out

Write 4 - 6 notes here

- David this little boy goes hunting with his dad in the Crazies.
- When his father and him are going back to the car, the boy went for a drink from the stream. When the boy kneels down, he gets bit by a baby cub hiding in the snow.
- While the kids hand was bleeding they were fleeing from wherever the cubs mother would be. WHile running the father helped the son into a tree and tried giving hima gun for his own protection. The attempt of giving the gunn to his kid ended with him getting shot in the leg.
- The rest of the story is of the father and son trying to find their way back for safety and medical care.

Secret Ingredients:

"It rose suddenly with a high squealing growl and whirled its head like a snake and snapped."

An example of an Iron Chef Lesson slide using the short story "Walking Out" by David Quammen.

In short, with EduProtocols you have to start somewhere. But you don't have to eat the elephant simultaneously, and you surely won't understand the entire Grand Canyon with one glance. So, try these out, and after a few reps, add another EduProtocol. By the time the semester ends, you'll have a toolkit you feel comfortable using, students will feel confident in how to "do the thing," and your planning time will be cut to a fraction of what it was before.

Other Classic EduProtocols

The number of EduProtocols used in classrooms is constantly growing, but there are always a few classics that have become favorites and continue to lead the pack in usability. Here are a few you might not be familiar with that aren't discussed further in this book. For more information on them and many others, consider looking at the rest of the series of EduProtocols. There is also an ever-developing playlist of tutorials on my YouTube page.

Parafly EduProtocol

Students need explicit training in summarizing and paraphrasing, as they frequently confuse the two skills. Many adults do this in conversation. Think of when someone says, "Let me paraphrase this for you" when, in fact, they're shortening the information and distilling it into its main points.

Summarizing involves condensing a piece of writing or speech into a shorter form while retaining the main ideas and essential details. It provides a brief overview of a text or speech and can be helpful in quickly conveying critical points to someone else.

Paraphrasing, on the other hand, involves expressing the ideas in a text or speech in your own words. It is a way of rephrasing the original material while maintaining the same meaning and elements. Paraphrasing can help you demonstrate your understanding of the material and express your ideas about a topic.

By understanding the difference between these two concepts, and better yet, why to employ one over the other, students are better prepared for more advanced writing. The use of paraphrasing and summarizing increases their ability to write academically and integrate sources with style.

Parafly is an EduProtocol that practices this essential skill with lots of reps.

To run Parafly, provide students with a simple resource. This could be a paragraph, speech, video, or other material. Then ask them to do the following:

1. Engage with the original text or speech carefully and try to understand its main points.

2. Take notes on the ideas and important details, using your own words as much as possible.

3. Review your list of details and ideas and rewrite them in your own words.

4. Check your paraphrase against the original text to ensure that you have accurately conveyed all ideas and have not copied any phrases or sentences verbatim.

5. Paste your paraphrased work into a program like Socrative, a shared document, or any other collaborative platform we are using as a class for this protocol.

6. As a class, let's look at the paraphrased work. Look for instances where word constructions are too similar to the original text or where additional information needs to be included.

7. As an extension, copy one of the examples and paraphrase or revise it.

Paraphrasing can be a challenging skill to master, but it is an important part of academic writing and can help students to develop their critical thinking and communication skills. I like to use Parafly to switch between the modes of summarizing and paraphrasing so students internalize their differences. I'll often give a student a resource and have them quote, summarize, and paraphrase it all in one go!

Jake

I like having students quote, summarize, and paraphrase all at the same time to solidify the differences between them.

3x Challenge EduProtocol

The 3x Challenge EduProtocol is a writing activity that tasks students with writing about a prompt in three different styles. This might be points of view (first, second, third), types of writing (narrative, persuasive, informative), or even genres (romance, comedy, horror). This activity is often done as a Google Slides presentation.

The 3x Challenge can help students to develop their writing skills and to think critically about different perspectives and viewpoints. It can also be a fun and engaging way to practice writing in differing styles, thus building flexibility. It can be fun to use things that aren't fiction or story based. Requiring students to write from three points of view about something like "What is the rhetorical situation of X" requires them to think deeply about the topic.

3X POV   Character:Dede

Think of the sister listed. Write 3-4 sentences as if introducing her to the author in an interview for the book from three points of view.

POV: How would she introduce herself?	POV: How would people of her community introduce her?	POV: How would people of the government introduce her?
She would introduce herself by telling you her name. She would then tell you about her day. Maybe tell you a few stories.	They would introduce her as a strong, willed spirit, independent because she has to be. She is also kind and shy. She believes to stand for something and carries that out with her actions.	They would introduce her and her family as trouble making; a powerful force. They would probably find Dede to be less forceful against the government than her other sisters.

A student example of a 3x POV slide using the novel *In the Time of the Butterflies* by Julia Alvarez.

To complete the 3x Challenge EduProtocol, follow these steps:

1. Provide students with a prompt, such as a picture, a video, a short story, a news article, or a real-life situation, and ask students to write about it in three different styles. Use a presentation slide or other doc format.

Jake

There's also a growing list of tutorials on my YouTube page. Check it out! There's new content coming all the time. Make sure you subscribe so you don't miss out. www.tinyurl.com/EduPtutorials

2. Direct students first to write about the prompt in their most comfortable style.

3. Next, ask students to write about the same prompt in the next two styles.

This EduProtocol can easily be remixed into different styles. One widespread usage is known as 5x, and instead of three points of view, students respond to a prompt in five techniques: descriptive, narrative, persuasive, creative, and compare/contrast.

Chapter 2

EduProtocols and Artificial Intelligence

As we navigate the dynamic landscape of twenty-first-century education, we increasingly encounter the intersection of innovative pedagogical practices and cutting-edge technology. One such collaboration is the integration of EduProtocols with artificial intelligence (AI) tools in the classroom. Throughout this book, I want to highlight how the fusion of these two powerful resources can revolutionize the teaching and learning experience.

EduProtocols are versatile lesson frames designed to deliver content in engaging, predictable, and effective ways to students. These frameworks, adaptable to any subject or grade level, empower teachers to deliver content in a supportive and creative environment. Each EduProtocol provides a structured approach to teaching and learning, with opportunities for collaboration, critical thinking, and mastery of academic content.

On the other side of the equation, we have AI. AI technologies, particularly language models such as generative pre-trained transformer models (GPT), can understand, generate, and analyze natural language text. These AI models can assist educators in providing personalized feedback, developing engaging prompts, and fostering interactive discussions in the blink of an eye. Gone are the hours scouring the internet for just the right text.

When EduProtocols and AI are brought together, the possibilities are boundless. Let's explore a few examples:

- Fast and Curious Remixes: In this EduProtocol, students participate in quick, low-stakes quizzes to reinforce learning. With AI, teachers can generate a diverse array of questions, ensuring that each quiz is fresh and

Marlena

AI is an effective tool that can help teachers address students' individual needs. Try inserting a passage and adjusting the reading level for your struggling readers! Same content, easier read!

engaging. AI models can also analyze student responses, providing insights into knowledge gaps and areas for re-teaching.

- Iron Chef Lesson: Inspired by the fast-paced cooking show, this EduProtocol encourages students to work in teams to create informative slides. By leveraging AI-generated content, students can enrich their presentations with accurate and well-organized information, enhancing the quality of their final product.

- Cyber Sandwich: This is an EduProtocols take on the classic Think-Pair-Share, and it's taken from *The EduProtocol Field Guide: Book 1*. Cyber Sandwich invites students to discuss, synthesize, and summarize the content. With AI's natural language processing capabilities, teachers can create specific resources for the lesson. Students can receive real-time feedback on their written reflections, allowing them to refine their thoughts and effectively communicate their understanding.

- Random Emoji Power Paragraph: In this EduProtocol, students use emojis as prompts to craft meaningful paragraphs. AI models can add an extra layer of creativity to this activity by generating unique and thought-provoking emoji-based prompts and offering feedback on the coherence and style of students' writing. For more about this EduProtocol, see *The EduProtocols Field Guide: Book 2* or the remixes below.

It's important to note that integrating AI with EduProtocols aims only to supplement the human touch in education. AI is a valuable tool that amplifies the impact of EduProtocols, allowing educators to provide personalized and differentiated instruction and students to explore their creativity and critical thinking.

And now, meet your friendly guide to the world of artificial intelligence in education—our little AI bot! As you journey through this book, our tech-savvy companion will pop up with innovative and practical ideas for seamlessly integrating AI into your teaching practices. Whether by offering tips on personalized feedback,

suggesting secret ingredients for the Iron Chef Lesson, or generating creative writing prompts, this charming bot has you covered.

The fusion of EduProtocols and AI offers boundless opportunities to revolutionize teaching and learning. And as you embrace the future of education with your trusty robot companion by your side, just remember: even this chapter was written with a little AI magic! That's right, your friendly neighborhood AI language model has been your author for this chapter all along. Who knew robots could have such a way with words? Wishing you an electrifying journey ahead, full of bright bytes and clever circuits!

Chapter 3
A Note on EduProtocols and Universal Design for Learning

EduProtocols are not just innovative teaching frameworks; they are infused naturally with Universal Design for Learning (UDL) principles. From the outset, these frameworks are crafted with the diverse needs of all learners in mind. By offering multiple means of engagement, representation, and expression, EduProtocols seamlessly align with UDL's inclusive approach to education. Each one showcases the importance of flexibility and student-centered learning, accommodating various learning styles and preferences. These approaches include diverse selection and presentation of resources—whether written, visual, or auditory—and encourage students to engage kinesthetically, logically, and creatively, both individually and in collaboration with peers.

In this book, while I won't repeat UDL's principles in each chapter, it's important to recognize that they are the bedrock upon which EduProtocols are built. I began by writing a segment on how each EduProtocol exhibited UDL principles, but as I got a few chapters in, I realized there was no way I was going to be that repetitive! "Sorry, Jon. Not doing it." As you explore each protocol, you'll see how they inherently embrace and promote varied pathways for learning, ensuring that education is accessible, engaging, and effective for every student. This introductory understanding of UDL's integration is key to appreciating the full potential of Edu-Protocols in transforming classroom learning. I encourage you to allow for even greater flexibility and creativity as you adapt and shift each one to your own setting and style. Teach according to the people you're with and the moment you're in, not according to some made-up ideal that I've created in writing this book. Write it. Talk it. Draw it. Imagine it. Walk it. Do all the things.

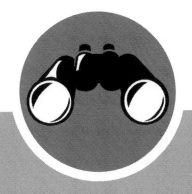

SECTION 2

A Guide to New EduProtocols

Chapter 4
Wicked Hydra EduProtocol

Wicked Hydra tackles the common issue of surface-level learning by asking students to actively collaborate against it with deep questioning. By encouraging students to build upon questions like branches in a mind map, we can foster deeper thinking that moves quickly beyond simple answers. This collaborative approach harnesses the power of diverse perspectives to move past initial assumptions, reveal nuanced connections, and ultimately uncover new ideas and ways of exploration. Far too often, we solidify students' thinking too quickly. Wicked Hydra is a way to leave their door to wonder open a little longer.

While seemingly simple, Wicked Hydra's true strength lies in its ability to unlock curiosity and expand the joy of questioning, and it propels students on a path that accesses prior knowledge, develops and encourages lateral thinking, and enhances a nuanced understanding of the topic at hand.

Academic Goals

Through successful implementation of Wicked Hydra, students should:

- Develop more profound thinking around questions, driving deeper inquiry
- Foster a sense of curiosity around a subject without solidifying their thinking too quickly

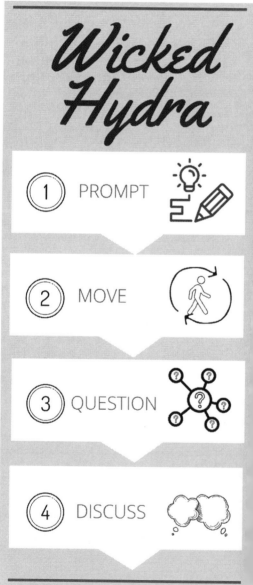

- Access prior knowledge and bring it into the forefront
- Be encouraged to think laterally

Teacher Big Ideas

- Keep this activity as simple and unstructured as possible. The purpose is to explore. It is meant to be expansive, not contractive.
- Focus on the process rather than an end product. The goal is connection, not production. If you need a product, some variations are given.
- Agree on non-closure. Sometimes it's OK to just ask a question without needing it to be answered.

Prepare for the Activity

1. Obtain paper of some sort. It could be poster-sized sheets or standard copier paper. Refrain from running this Edu-Protocol digitally, as the graphic and spatial nature of the project is part of the learning.
2. Prepare an opening resource. This might be a thought-provoking image, a quote from the content, or a good open-ended question that will drive deeper inquiry. The intent is to encourage students to think deeply and question a topic.
3. Decide how many questions each student will be responsible for exploring. Typically, three to five is a good place for most sessions. Too few and you only get surface-level thinking; too many and you belabor the review.

Instructions

1. Divide the class into manageable groups of four or five.
2. Give each group something to write on with the opening prompt on it. Say you're reading *The Little Prince* and you

want students to think more critically about the symbolic characters in the story. You could use an image of a rose or a fox, or you could use a quote about the desert or an interesting starter thought.

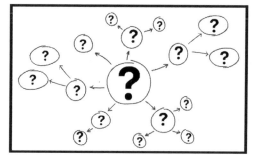

3. Instruct each group to create the first tier of a tree diagram by writing questions that advance or further clarify the original resource. Consider using a questioning matrix to help them form different types of questions. I like to sometimes give them starter stems based on the Depth of Knowledge scale or something from Bloom's taxonomy. For example: What does the Little Prince want?

    ▶ Is he looking for a friend who treats him well?

    ▶ Does he need to escape the rose?

    ▶ Is he bored on his planet?

    ▶ Is he afraid the baobab trees will destroy his asteroid?

4. Instruct students to move around the room individually and write questions on the other groups' papers. Each new question should build on the questions from Step 3 that

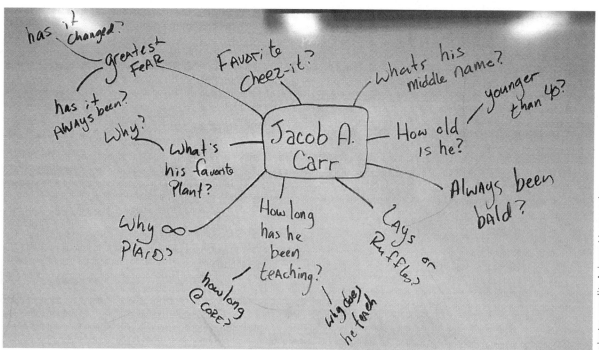

Consider using the teacher's name as a way to teach Wicked Hydra.
Then, let students ask questions about you!

branch off the original opening question. This creates the hydra effect. Each student should write at least one question per paper, but they may offer as many as instructed.

5. Once students have finished offering questions, give them a few moments to review their original group's paper and discuss the questions posed by their classmates.

6. Give each student a 3x5 card and have them silently revisit each station, recording one question they think they can answer on their 3x5 card (one question per station).

7. Students return to their desks and pick one question to find the answer for and add a picture to. (A Padlet Thin Slide is particularly useful for this digital approach.) Once all the students have solved one question, the teacher can simply hit the Present arrow in Padlet, and each student can share their question and answer in about four seconds apiece. Alternatively, for a non-digital approach, the teacher can use 3x5 cards that students turn in as an exit ticket.

Emily

I was homeschooled for most of my childhood, so I didn't have many opportunities to hear other students' questions. Wicked Hydra is a great activity to learn from one another and gain new perspectives.

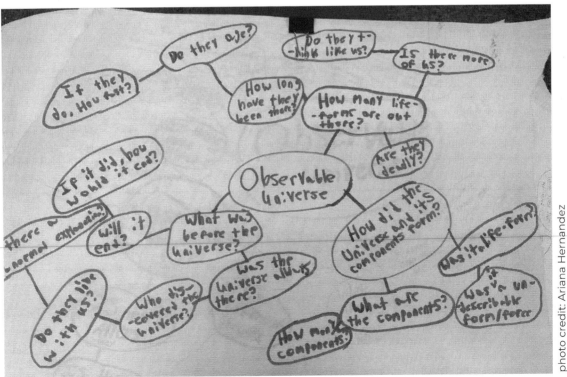

photo credit: Ariana Hernandez

Here, students are using Wicked Hydra in a middle school science class!

8. As an optional closure, students answer this question: "What new idea did you uncover today?" You might choose to have them respond to the question or just record the question itself.

Key Points to Remember

- Keep this activity as simple and unstructured as possible. The purpose is to explore. It is meant to be expansive, not contractive.

- Focus on the process rather than an end product. The goal is exploration, not production. If you need a product, some variations are given.

- Agree on non-closure. Sometimes it's OK to just ask a question without needing it to be answered.

- Students have often been taught *not* to question things. It might take a few rounds before they feel comfortable and confident posing big or creative questions. It could be helpful to discuss various questioning matrixes and strategies before subsequent attempts in order to help them form questions that go beyond who, what, when, where, and why. I've also found that explicitly teaching students the difference between open-ended questions and closed ones is beneficial to get above first-tier, foundational questioning and into deeper, lateral-thinking areas.

Variations

Discussion Prep

Use Wicked Hydra as a way for students to prepare questions for an upcoming Socratic seminar or discussion. At the end of the Wicked Hydra session, direct students to write a thought-provoking question on a 3x5 card for the stack.

Use AI to automatically generate starting questions from assigned readings, ensuring students engage deeply with the text.

Essay Prep

After a Wicked Hydra session, have students trace a single line of questioning from the initial resource to the last tier, moving from the first question through all the follow-up ones. Use this line of questioning as the scaffold for a writing project where they do a whole-to-part deep dive, backing their claims with evidence along the way to build out an essay outline.

Chasm of Questions

Begin with multiple opening questions and allow space for lots of follow-up questions. This is a way to explore various aspects of a single subject. For example, you might explore multiple themes in a novel, numerous claims in a piece of rhetoric, or even something like the stages of cell division.

Evolving Hydra

Post large sheets of paper on the classroom wall during an entire unit of study with a critical opening question on each. Prompt students to perform a Wicked Hydra on those initial questions. Then, as students move through the course of study, give them a moment to update the Wicked Hydra posters as questions change or new questions emerge.

The Audit

After a Wicked Hydra session, allow students another few moments to review the questions posed on each group's paper and place a checkmark next to questions they consider necessary or exciting. Use these "greatest hits" as the basis of discussion.

Wagon Wheel

After a Wicked Hydra session, divide the last level of questions and pass each to a group. Give groups time to research and answer the questions using a Thick Slides EduProtocol. Students need to rewrite and edit the third-level questions so that they remain clear when disassociated from their parent questions.

Don't Forget the Pictures!

Images such as cartoons, paintings, and primary source documents make great starting points for Wicked Hydra. Just plop one down in the middle of the page and let the students start their questions.

Q&A Review

After students create Wicked Hydras, choose a day to have them go back and write answers to the questions, providing evidence. They could answer unanswered questions, refute something, or further develop the solutions provided by others.

AP Adaptation and Correlation to Enduring Understandings

When students practice open-ended questioning, they are given an opportunity to engage fully with both their peers and course texts. As a result, Wicked Hydra develops essential communication skills organically. Along the way, conversation prompts students to think differently about a topic, and building new questions encourages them to feel confident in their ideas while improving their critical thinking skills. The outcome is a deeper understanding of the resource.

Wicked Hydra can support any Enduring Understanding, depending on how you utilize it.

① BUILD

② PRINT

③ SHUFFLE

④ PLAY

Higher-order thinking skills like analysis and synthesis rely heavily on vocabulary and concept development, which are essential throughout the learning process. Most concepts are picked up unwittingly by children as a result of their constant interactions with spoken and written language. However, content-specific jargon isn't common enough in everyday usage for students to be familiar with it; that terminology needs to be taught.

Repuzzler gamifies vocabulary acquisition. Through the seemingly simple process of linking various aspects of a term to one another, this EduProtocol builds a deeper understanding of new vocabulary. We use a modified Frayer Model (a four-quadrant graphic organizer originally developed to deepen understanding of vocabulary) and add a little physical movement to help students quickly and deeply scaffold their learning of complex concepts. Once these new ideas are accessible, students can utilize them to understand increasingly complex skills and processes.

Academic Goals

Through successful implementation of Repuzzler, students should be able to:

- Define conceptual material and new vocabulary
- Memorize those definitions

Jon

The Frayer Model becomes collaborative and higher order while remaining low prep!

- Represent new material nonlinguistically
- Collaboratively reconstruct information
- Classify and correlate facets of information to build toward a greater understanding of course concepts

Teacher Big Ideas

- Repuzzler isn't an end goal but a repeatable tool for helping students build higher-order thinking skills. For example, it would be unnecessarily burdensome for a student to analyze a speech's rhetoric without first understanding what *rhetorical* means.
- By helping students to build vocabulary before they need to use it, the cognitive load is lightened, allowing students to focus more on the content than the process.
- This EduProtocol was developed for ELA, but it quickly exploded across grade levels and subjects when tested. Have fun! Share this EduProtocol with your colleagues in other departments.

Prepare for the Activity

1. Prepare a list of vocabulary.
2. Prepare a collaborative slide deck with each slide divided into four quadrants.
3. Populate each slide with one vocabulary word in the top right quadrant.
4. Decide how students will split up and complete the vocabulary words.
5. Assign the shared deck to students.

Jake

How about a template deck?

Instructions

1. Students begin by completing the quadrants of the deck according to the vocabulary word on a given slide. In the

Jon

I love how Jake makes the kids think his Repuzzler is a standard Frayer on paper and then gets out scissors and chops it up!

four quadrants of their slide, they 1) add a definition, 2) add the term being learned, 3) provide an antonym or use the vocabulary word in a sentence, and 4) insert an image or icon representing the word.

2. Print the deck and cut it into four separate pieces along the lines.

3. Pull out the vocabulary word quadrants and place them all faceup on desks or tables around the room. Part of the fun is moving!

4. Shuffle the remaining pieces and distribute them evenly to the class.

5. Time the students as they rebuild their slides by placing their quadrants together with the appropriate vocabulary word.

6. Repeat!

Key Points to Remember

- This one is meant to be fun; let it be. Play music while students are racing toward a better score—my classes like a disco playlist.

- Build stamina by first using a shorter vocabulary list.

- This activity can be an excellent "hidden curriculum" moment, meaning it's a culture-building moment that has nothing to do with content. The first round can be messy and a little chaotic. Use that time to debrief on what went well and what got in the way. Then, as students workshop how to rebuild their slides, they will learn to interact efficiently and politely, use safe indoor pathways, and observe other unspoken classroom culture lessons.

image	word or concept
definition	antonym or usage

Here is a simple version of a Frayer Model for vocabulary. Cut it up, and you've got Repuzzler!

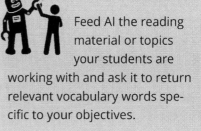

Feed AI the reading material or topics your students are working with and ask it to return relevant vocabulary words specific to your objectives.

Here is another version of a Frayer using different requirements (image, term, definition, trait)

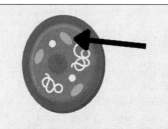

Mitochondria

the organelle found in most cells where cellular respiration and energy production take place

The mitochondria produces more than 90% of a cells energy

Variations

Rack and Stack with Fast and Curious (#FastAndCurious)

Before completing the Repuzzler deck, have students review the same list of vocabulary via Fast and Curious. Instead of reviewing missed words, begin Repuzzler immediately. Then, alternate rounds of Repuzzler and Fast and Curious.

Thin Slide Study Guide (#TSSGRepuzzler)

Day 1

1. Begin by asking students to choose one word from the Repuzzler deck, or assign it to them. If you need to, double or triple the terms to make enough so each student has one slide.

2. Students complete the definition portion of the slide.

3. The deck gets presented to the class as part of Thin Slide Study Guide. When a student's slide shows up, they deliver the new information they have provided on that slide aloud.

Day 2

1. Students complete the remainder of the slide by finding an antonym, using it in a sentence, and selecting an image or icon representing the vocabulary word.

2. Present the Repuzzler deck again to the class. When a student's slide shows up, they deliver the new information aloud.

Day 3

1. Proceed to play the Repuzzler game as outlined in Steps 2 to 5 of the instructions section above.

Ikonic Mode (#IkonicVocab)

You can use Repuzzler in conjunction with the Ikonic EduProtocol by having students use their crafted icons as the visual image for Repuzzler.

Jake

How about a template deck?

Day 1

1. Students complete the definition portion of their slide.

2. Present the deck to the class. When a student's slide shows up, they deliver the new information aloud.

Day 2

1. Students complete the Ikonic EduProtocol.

Day 3

1. Students complete the Repuzzler deck by adding their Ikonic image and the antonym or usage in a sentence.

Day 4

1. Proceed with standard Repuzzler gameplay as outlined in Steps 2 to 5 in the instructions section above.

Digital Mode

This EduProtocol works great if you teach online or want to try this out online! A TikTok user (@gingerhalfling) shared the Card Sort function on Desmos as a great option for Repuzzler. With this mode, the teacher makes one vocabulary set and pushes it out to students. That way, each student can have their own practice set. Desmos can also check for correctness.

Ragnarok Unleashed Mode (#RagnarokUnleashed)

Rack and Stack, Repuzzler, Ikonic, and Fast and Curious EduProtocols make for an epic week of vocabulary development. Use the Ikonic EduProtocol to create images, build the Repuzzler deck, and alternate Repuzzler's game mode with Fast and Curious.

AP Adaptation and Correlation to Enduring Understandings

Repuzzler is a highly permutable EduProtocol. It has been used successfully from kindergarten through university courses. Educators can increase the complexity of the Frayer Model to meet the zone of proximal development for their students. Consider having students create a deck specific to their needs as an AP adaptation.

Repuzzler can support any Enduring Understanding, depending on how you utilize it.

Ikonic

1. PLAN
2. PRIME
3. SIMPLIFY
4. PLAY

Vocabulary development is essential for skill learning and cognitive development. In some philosophies, our thoughts are the product of our language; the more exact our language, the more we can hone our thinking from pictorial to linguistic knowledge. It is the foundation for understanding new concepts and ideas, and a strong vocabulary is necessary for adequate comprehension and communication.

Ikonic helps students understand the cognitive and non-linguistic aspects of vocabulary and concepts. Investing extra time in Ikonic will yield significant benefits as students become more adept at manipulating their knowledge. By cognitive aspects, I mean comprehension of words through their connections, uses, and subtleties rather than just memorization. Non-linguistic learning involves engaging with visual and sensory experiences, which enhances understanding and memory. This holistic approach to vocabulary equips students to use their knowledge in diverse and creative ways, making their learning more dynamic and applicable in real-world situations.

Academic Goals

Through successful implementation of Ikonic, students should be able to:

- Develop new conceptual material, such as vocabulary and ideas

- Represent course concepts nonlinguistically
- Collaboratively construct shared schemata
- Classify and correlate facets of information to achieve a greater understanding of course material

Teacher Big Ideas

Developing a solid foundation of terminology will yield more significant results when students need to use terms for higher-order projects and understanding. For example, in analyzing fiction, understanding the idea of symbolism can deepen students' understanding of *The Great Gatsby* as they begin to see significance in the green light. In rhetoric, a foundational knowledge of ethos and its purpose helps students analyze Churchill's process of credibility-building in his Blood, Toil, Tears, and Sweat speech. These types of terms help students unlock deeper and nuanced analyses.

Prepare for the Activity

1. Develop and introduce a foundation of iconography and how ideas are transferred using imagery and shared meaning.

2. Begin to develop a toolkit, or lexicon, of images and icons that are understood by the class. For example, a pyramid of three dots means *therefore*, and a thumbs-down could mean *no*. Consider using tools such as Flaticon and the Noun Project or other icon-based resources.

3. Identify a list of words or concepts for students to learn.

4. Have scratch paper on hand for initial drafts of the exercise.

5. Have ample 3-by-5 notecards (or similar) on hand for students. They'll need to make plenty of mistakes without feeling like they must get things perfect the first time. I've found that sturdier paper stock is beneficial for longer-term usage.

Instructions for Creation

1. Assign a word or concept to each student or group.
2. Give students time to draft a single icon representing the word or concept. Then, give them resources to draw from existing icons that they can combine in new ways. This icon becomes the *Prime*.

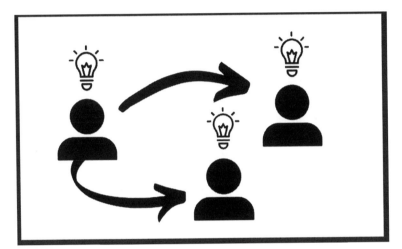

Here is a "prime" example of the term Argument. See how it depicts the idea being delivered to other people?

3. Once students draft a Prime icon, they draw a secondary set of icons (*Expanded* icons) that further explain the Prime. Finally, they compile multiple icons together to explain their assigned word or concept in pictures.

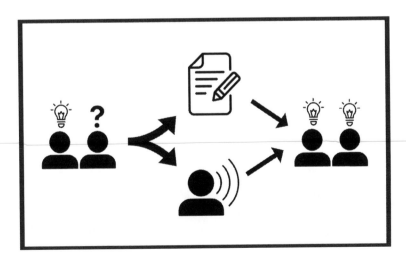

Here is the expanded example of Argument. See how the idea, believed by one party, is shared via speaking or writing and then believed by both parties?

You can ask a GPT model to suggest icons for anything. Sometimes students just need a little push in the right direction.

4. Ask groups to share their work with each other to double-check that their icons are comprehensible.

5. When they're happy with their Prime and Expanded icons, have students create their 3-by-5 card by drawing the Prime icon on one side and the Expanded icons on the other. Next, they write the term or concept in a corner small enough to be covered by a finger easily.

Variations for Play

GroupThink

1. Offer a list of the terms or concepts to the class.

2. Each student or group shares a Prime icon without explaining its referent.

3. The class tries to correlate each Prime icon with its correct referent from the list of possible terms.

4. If they can't get it, the student or group presents its Expanded icons, and the class attempts to correlate the icons to the term again.

"OK, but Why?"

Students must recognize the Prime and Expanded icons and be able to explain how the icons signify the definition of the term or concept.

Round Robin

1. After the full set of Ikonic cards is created, number each card and lay them all out on a series of desks.

2. Students can gallery walk silently from card to card, writing down their guesses about which concept correlates to which numbered card.

Fast and Curious Style

Digitize the icons and put them into Gimkit or another online quiz option for review by the class.

Repuzzler Style

Use the icons as one or multiple quadrants of the Repuzzler Edu-Protocol.

Key Points to Remember

- While rewarding and highly beneficial, the Ikonic Edu-Protocol requires a lot of thinking. Start slow! Begin with only a few concepts and work as a single group. Once students understand the process of the EduProtocol, they'll enjoy the challenge of completing it alone or with a smaller group.

- Think of the Prime icon as the more challenging signifier of the concept and the Expanded icons as the more accessible explanations of it.

- Spending a little time developing the skill of seeing things as icons can benefit students in the long term not only by deepening their vocabulary, but also by helping them hone the skill of thinking pictorially. Visual thinking enhances memory retention and fosters complex idea comprehension. Begin this process slowly by creating simple icons for everyday items and functions. Think of this activity as a stripped-down Pictionary where you try to use as few images as possible while still relating concepts legibly. As students progress, this foundational practice can evolve into synthesis and recall of abstract concepts through visual representation. These skills prove advantageous in problem-solving, creativity, and lateral thinking across disciplines.

- Reinforce that students represent the *meaning* of the word, not the word itself. For example, when my students were explaining the concept of anchoring bias through Ikonic, many of them wanted to use the image of a ship's anchor, but that doesn't illuminate the definition.

AP Adaptation and Correlation to Enduring Understandings

According to Robert Marzano and John Hattie, nonlinguistic representations are huge for student recall and conceptual understanding—but we keep instructing students to write sentences to define words. Make your AP vocab iconic with Ikonic.

Developing a solid word sense around terms and concepts addresses all Enduring Understandings.

Marlena

UDL is a powerful motivator for students that will shift the ownership of learning from teacher to student. Incorporate this approach with Ikonic to deepen vocabulary comprehension and foster creative, dynamic learning.

Chapter 7
AnnoTwist EduProtocol

(1) ANNOTATE

(2) FRAYER

(3) ANALYZE

(4) PRODUCE

By examining style closely through the AnnoTwist EduProtocol, students learn to succinctly describe and understand a text's structure and the prevailing logic of it. This method does a great job of encouraging close reading by identifying specific organizational strategies such as narration, description, and argumentation, thus allowing students to unravel how a text is crafted and how its content works internally.

While AnnoTwist was designed around the modes of development used to classify rhetorical writing strategies like narration, description, and argumentation, it works perfectly with a whole catalog of styles and techniques such as persuasive, expository, and narrative as well as literary devices such as metaphor, simile, and irony.

Academic Goals

Through successful implementation of AnnoTwist, students should be able to:

- Recognize specific styles and techniques
- Interpret emotional effects of an author's choices on the reader
- Correlate rhetorical choices with the author's purpose for those choices
- Cite examples within a resource

Which literary device is the focus?--Flashback

Flashbacks are used to give context to the situation or let someone know its not the present.

Shivering in my blanket, eyes glued to the frosted window, the lonesome wail of a train rekindled a memory. That moonlit night, long past bedtime, when Papa took me owling...

The idea of nostalgia from the past can give people an emotional connection to the story and also give information about why the present is important

Many kids have most likely had similar experiences of late winter nights and staying up past bedtime.

An example from Maria Gallagher looking at the element of Flashbacks as seen in *Owl Moon* by Jane Yolen.

- Articulate an example passage's function within a resource
- Recognize modes of development and understand how they function in a larger argument

Teacher Big Ideas

- Based on a modified Iron Chef Lesson EduProtocol, students will learn an analysis format applicable to various styles and techniques.
- By identifying modes of development and how they function within a text, students will better understand how a text may be received by an audience and how it affects a rhetorical situation.
- By first deconstructing and examining the writing style of others, students will begin to internalize the process of developing style within their own writing.

- Work done in AnnoTwist translates to other EduProtocols, such as 8 p*ARTS and "We Have a Situation Here!" This will deepen students' understanding of a text and lead toward analytical writing.

Prepare for the Activity

1. Choose a resource that exemplifies the modes of development you aim to teach. This could be a reading selection, video, audio, comic, or artwork. Consider various media—short stories for literary devices, commercials for rhetorical elements, etc.

2. Before presenting the resource to students, identify and note the specific modes of development it demonstrates. This step ensures you are prepared to guide students in their analysis.

3. Depending on the format of your chosen resource (digital or analog), prepare an AnnoTwist slide deck or printed copy. Each slide or section should focus on one mode of development, with a clear title for each.

4. Provide students with access to the resource and the analysis tools. Ensure that they understand how to use these tools effectively for the activity.

Instructions

1. Instruct students to carefully examine the chosen resource either individually or in a group, identifying and annotating instances of various modes of development. These might include process, narration, description, exposition, argumentation, literary devices, cause and effect, etc.

2. Students should complete the AnnoTwist organizer for each identified mode of development. They will address the following points:

Jon

AnnoTwist is a ramped-up Iron Chef Lesson—advancing the Depth of Knowledge and academic complexity!

Jake

Here's a template deck!

▶ Identify the mode of development and its typical function in rhetoric.

▶ Locate and cite an example from the resource that demonstrates this mode.

▶ Analyze how the mode is used in the resource and infer the author's intent.

▶ Find and insert a meme, relevant GIF, or other image that represents the emotional impact of the mode on the audience, explaining the likely reaction.

3. Students should title each page or slide with the mode of development they are analyzing and repeat the process for each assigned mode.

4. Last, students should reflect on and articulate their reactions as audience members to the various rhetorical strategies employed in the resource

Key Points to Remember

This analytical work takes time to understand; don't rush the process. Instead, start by helping students to understand each mode of development before asking them to work with it in situ.

Variations

Literary Elements

AnnoTwist also works excellently in the context of literary analysis by allowing students to take a deeper look at literary elements such as plot, conflict, theme, setting, characters, etc.

Tell AI exactly what kind of reading material you want, and it will generate it for you! You can then ask it to shift the reading level to differentiate for students while still delivering the same material.

[Which literary element is the focus?]

[Which literary element is shown here and how does this strategy typically function in a piece of writing?]

[Provide an exemplary quote from the resource with citation]

[How does this literary element function specifically in this resource and why might the author have employed its usage?]

[Insert a .gif/meme/image that shows the emotions evoked in the audience. Explain why might they react this way.]

Solo

A single student completes the assignment for a given focus style or technique. Divide different modes of development across the class for a single resource, then have students report on what they discover.

4-Pass Twist

Perform this variation first on paper before trying it digitally. One student or group sets up a quote from the resource and then passes it to another student or group, who decides which mode that quote exhibits. Next, students pass the quotation and mode pairing to another student or group, who describes the function of the mode in the passage. After one last pass, a final student or group explains potential emotional reactions to the quote.

Full Twist

In this exercise, each group is responsible for analyzing a specific literary style and documenting their findings on four separate

3-by-5 note cards, with each card representing a different aspect of the original AnnoTwist analysis. This variation replaces the single four-segment slide with individual note cards for each segment. After the groups have completed their cards, all cards are collected, shuffled, and redistributed randomly among the class. Students engage in a group discussion to piece together the cards into complete sets according to the literary styles they represent. To avoid students identifying the sets by handwriting—a skill at which they are notably adept—ensure variety in handwriting within each group. This activity can also be carried out digitally, with students creating their analyses one day and then printing, cutting, and physically exchanging the sections the next, using the provided template. The Full Twist fosters a deeper understanding of how quotations can exemplify multiple literary styles and encourages debate over their diverse applications.

Modification for Middle Grades

- Focus on appropriate content-level skills, such as compare and contrast, sentence length, construction, etc.
- Use AnnoTwist to analyze literary elements with prompts such as:
  - ▶ Find a quote that describes how a character thinks.
  - ▶ What does this quote tell us about the character's inner thoughts and motives?
  - ▶ How does this way of thinking function in the world? How does it change how the character makes decisions in the novel?
  - ▶ What emotions might these decisions evoke in the character? What about how other characters react to them?

ELL Tips

- Focus heavily on explaining the modes of development and provide definitions and examples to refer to as students move into the material.
- Use resource material that links to study topics in other classes. This action helps an emerging bilingual student to incorporate topic-specific vocabulary.
- Bilingualism is the goal. Consider providing the resource in both the student's native and second language for reference.

AP Adaptation and Correlation to Enduring Understandings

The AnnoTwist EduProtocol excels in fostering AP-level competencies, particularly in analyzing rhetorical style, claims, and evidence. Its targeted approach sharpens students' ability to dissect authorial choices, understand reasoning, and evaluate the organization of texts. It's especially effective in elucidating the function of narrative elements, prompting students to articulate the roles and impact of characters, settings, and plot structures. Moreover, AnnoTwist encourages in-depth examination of the narrator or speaker's perspective and the strategic use of word choice, imagery, and symbols. This tool is adept at developing students' proficiency in these areas, aligning with AP standards and advancing their capacity for nuanced literary and rhetorical analysis.

Chapter 8
Claim Jumper EduProtocol

In our digital age, where data abounds and assertions fly, the ability to sift through claims and weigh evidence is not just an academic exercise but a vital life skill. The Claim Jumper EduProtocol is designed to hone this very skill, ensuring students are not merely passive recipients of information but active evaluators of the strength and validity of arguments. It's about staking a claim on the truth by assessing the merit of textual arguments and the robustness of their underpinning evidence.

Understanding how individual claims support the controlling thesis is crucial in this process. Each claim acts as a building block, contributing to the overall structure of the argument. The controlling thesis serves as the backbone, the central idea that all claims must prove and support. As students learn to evaluate how each claim substantiates the thesis, they gain a deeper appreciation for the intricate craft of argumentation.

Drawing inspiration from the days of the Old West, the Claim Jumper metaphor encapsulates the spirit of this EduProtocol. Just as claim jumpers would rush to assert ownership over valuable land, students dive into texts to extract valuable claims and evidence. They assess the worth of each claim as if weighing nuggets of gold, considering the richness of the evidence and the potential for counterclaims—turning the classroom into a lively assay office where the value of ideas is tested and debated.

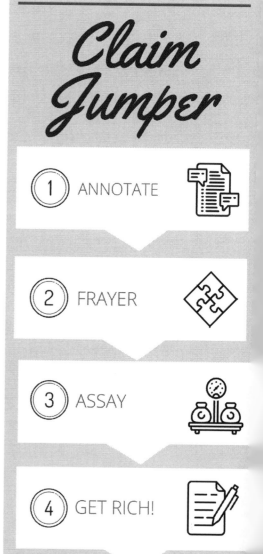

Claim Jumper

1. ANNOTATE
2. FRAYER
3. ASSAY
4. GET RICH!

The Claim Jumper EduProtocol is invaluable, not merely for the academic rigor it instills but for its role in cultivating discerning readers and articulate participants in the marketplace of ideas. It teaches students to navigate rhetoric with a critical eye, ensuring they can recognize a genuine claim from fool's gold, and it helps them understand how a series of well-founded claims build up to reinforce the controlling thesis, laying the groundwork for thoughtful, informed argumentation.

Academic Goals

Through successful implementation of Claim Jumper, students should be able to:

- Identify textual claims
- Identify and evaluate evidence
- Find alternative evidence that supports central claims
- Pose counterarguments
- Weigh the overall worth of the claims in terms of the evidence provided

Teacher Big Ideas

- Based on an advanced version of the classic Frayer Model, students should be able to adapt to the process of Claim Jumper with very little how-to instruction, allowing more time for exploring course content.
- Students determine how claims function in a larger body of work by identifying, examining, and deconstructing those claims.
- By analyzing claims in source texts, students will begin to internalize the process of developing claims in their writing.
- The skills honed through the Claim Jumper EduProtocol extend to other EduProtocols like Walk the Line, Thin Slides, and AnnoTwist, enhancing students' grasp of criti-

Jake

You might remember the Frayer Model as that four-square chart where you dissect new concepts. It's like a little brainstorming session on paper. It helps you sort out and really get the gist of what you're learning.

Jon

If we don't teach kids with a lot of reps before a debate or Socratic seminar, the outcomes can be low level and stilted. Claim Jumper creates a high-energy, high-rep situation to truly build skills kids can wield, so they're not just repeating or reading off a card.

Jake

How about a template deck?

cal thinking and argumentative writing. These protocols collaboratively reinforce how to dissect and engage with complex ideas, effectively shaping students' analytical abilities. Claim Jumper serves not just as an analytical exercise but also as a foundational step for writing, helping students organize their thoughts and structure their arguments before they begin composing their essays.

Prepare for the Activity

1. Link a rhetorical resource (reading selection, video, audio, comic, piece of artwork, etc.) to the assignment.

2. Preview the resource to determine the number of claims it presents.

3. Prepare a template deck for students with one slide for each claim that students will identify over the course of the EduProtocol.

4. Provide a link to the rhetorical resource in the template deck.

5. Assign the slide deck and individual claims to students or groups via your preferred method.

6. Create an empty, shared slide deck where students will compile their final slide with their group members.

Instructions

1. Begin by presenting students with your chosen resource. Then, depending on the complexity of the resource and the students' skill levels, you may want to incorporate close reading or other annotation techniques prior to Claim Jumper to ensure the resource is well understood.

2. Direct students to begin by working through the resource, finding its claims and adding each to the middle of a prepared slide. The rest of that slide will revolve around that specific claim.

[What evidence is given to support this claim?]

[What effect does this claim have on the controlling thesis? How does it advance the argument?]

[Copy a claim from the original text into this box.
Cite where to find it in the document (paragraph, line, etc.)]

[Find or create another piece of evidence NOT found in the original resource material that supports this claim. Don't forget to cite your source.]

[How could you counter this claim?]

Jacob Carr, @MrCarrOnTheWeb 2021

3. For each claim, students answer the prompts in each quadrant of the slide:

    ▶ What evidence is given to support this claim?

    ▶ What effect does this claim have on the controlling thesis? How does it advance the argument?

    ▶ Find or create another piece of evidence *not* found in the original resource material that supports this claim. Don't forget to cite your source.

    ▶ How could you counter this claim?

4. Now, it's time to take it to the assay office. Once students have mined the resource text for its gold—its claims—it's time to weigh it and see just how good the claims are. Students will categorize each claim's strengths, weaknesses, and neutral points in the boxes provided.

5. Now it's time to "Get Rich" and turn the resource text into treasure! Direct students to analyze the text's claims in terms of how effective and how well supported they are. How could the author have made those claims even better or added to them? There are many ways students can show their analysis—by writing, creating a video response, or

Jake

In the Claim Jumper EduProtocol, the assay office metaphor represents the critical analysis phase where students assess the value of their extracted claims. Like gold assayers who tested nuggets for authenticity and value, students scrutinize each claim to determine its argumentative weight—its persuasive power, potential flaws, and areas of ambiguity—carefully sorting them to establish their contribution to the essay's central thesis.

ASSAY OFFICE

How pure is the gold?

Now that you've mined the gold, it's time to weigh it out and see just how good the claims are. In the boxes below, categorize the strengths, weaknesses, and neutral points of the claims.

STRONG	NEUTRAL	WEAK

By sorting claims by how effective they are, students begin to see that not all claims are alike in leading logically toward their conclusion.

working toward other outcomes. So, give students the choice. And as a unifying feature, have students include an image or GIF that shows how happy they would be with the rhetorical treasure they have found.

Key Points to Remember

- Students may need help discerning a text's claims. Therefore, ensure they are on the right track before they get to work on developing their analysis of the claim they choose to examine. Consider offering structured time for students to review the resource and pull out the claims before diving deeper into the work. Then, provide real-time feedback and collaborate as a whole class by posting students' claims in a shared Thin Slides deck.

- Help students to assess source texts as credible or non-credible when finding their evidence to support a given claim.
- Structure this activity with scaffolding to ensure student success. Examining every claim for an entire rhetorical essay could be challenging for some students. Begin small, go slow, and move from success to success to build competencies.

Variations

Group Iron Chef Lesson

A great way to scaffold this activity is to give one claim to each group. Group members then divide the work with each member taking a quadrant to answer or moving through them together in discussion. When each group finishes, they should report their findings to the class. Then, the entire class can discuss how the text's collective claims work together.

Exquisite Corpse Model

- This version should be organized as a series of rounds. Begin by splitting your class into a number of groups equal to the number of claims in the resource. Then, give each group a beginning claim. Groups answer one quadrant in the first round, then pass their first claim to the next group for the next round. In essence, the whole class works with a single quadrant per round but examines new claims each round. This version can be done on paper or digitally in a shared slide deck. The rounds go as follows:
  - ▶ Round 1: What evidence is given to support this claim?
  - ▶ Round 2: What effect does this claim have on the controlling thesis? How does it advance the overall argument?

Marlena

This kind of checking as you go will save time not only in grading but in keeping kids on track. A key ingredient for any EduProtocol. Get your weekends back!

Try feeding claims and a conclusion into a GPT model and ask it to analyze for logic and validity.

Jake

Exquisite Corpse was a Victorian-era parlor game where the guests drew a "monster" part by part until the end drawing was revealed. This is also fun to do with students!

- ▶ Round 3: Find or create another piece of evidence *not* found in the original resource material that supports this claim. Don't forget to cite your source.
  - ▶ Round 4: How could you counter this claim?
- Each group can examine a complete piece of rhetoric instead of a single claim. The group completes all quadrants in each round and then passes their text on to the next group. Over time, the claims add up to form a line of reasoning. Using resources on a similar topic is an excellent prewriting activity before students take a stance to defend the issue via writing or speaking.

Multiday Model

Do a single Claim Jumper slide each day for three days. On Day 4, complete the assay office and Get Rich slides. On Day 5, turn Get Rich into an introduction and conclusion. By the end, students will have drafted a five-paragraph essay that is ready to be edited! This method is much more structured than sending a rhetorical analysis assignment home for a week only to have kids complete it on the last day. Also, by giving students daily feedback on their analysis, the final products will be of much higher quality, and your grading time will go way down.

Construction

Claim Jumper also works as a graphic organizer for students to construct their arguments. After creating their controlling thesis, students write their claims before answering the quadrants to build their line of reasoning. Follow this format with the Multiday Model for even greater success!

Deeper Mining

As a writing exercise, direct students to compose an analysis of each claim as described in Claim Jumper. Focus on the relationships between the cells. Then, depending on students' prior knowl-

Emily

This is my favorite model because it provides me instant feedback to build on later. That way, when I'm working on finalization, I have some tips for moving forward!

edge and skills, add elements of how each cell in Claim Jumper relates to the rhetorical situation and modes of development.

Hive Mind Writing

- In this variation of the Claim Jumper EduProtocol, collaboration and role-switching are key components that enhance the learning experience. Initially, a selected group of students takes on the role of producers, diving into the heart of essay construction. They focus on outlining and drafting, harnessing skills sharpened by the protocol. Their counterparts, the *support team*, play a vital assisting role, providing research assistance, offering feedback, and serving as sounding boards to refine the producers' arguments.

- As the producers work on constructing their essays, they are encouraged to engage with the support team actively, seeking insights and clarifications to bolster their arguments and ensure alignment with the controlling thesis. The support team stands ready to pivot between research, editorial advice, and critical analysis, ensuring the producers have a robust foundation for their writing.

- After a set period, the students switch roles, allowing each participant to experience and practice the different aspects of essay production—both the analysis and construction phases. This dynamic approach not only encourages peer learning but also mirrors the real-world process of collaborative projects, where roles often shift and adapt to the project's needs. By engaging in both sides of the essay development process, students gain a comprehensive understanding of the elements that make up a strong, cohesive argument.

Modification for Middle Grades

- Adjust the number of claims used.
- Provide the claim and one or two other quadrants for a student and have them complete the missing information. Then, by rotating what you ask of the student, they'll practice all the skills covered by Claim Jumper in turn.
- Consider providing the quadrants as a list of discussion topics to be developed only orally.
- Scale your resource appropriately to the abilities of your students. If you're working with a group of students with a wide range, assigning differently leveled resources is an easy way to provide access.

ELL Tips

- Use resource material that links to study topics in other classes. For example, connect with the student's history teacher and use a primary source document being reviewed for that class. This action helps an emerging bilingual student to incorporate topic-specific vocabulary.
- Bilingualism is the goal. Consider providing the resource in both the student's native and second language for reference.

AP Adaptation and Correlation to Enduring Understandings

Classroom debates ignite critical thinking, but they're time-consuming and laborious to set up. Claim Jumper offers a streamlined alternative, packing the punch of debate into a compact, twenty-minute session. This efficient protocol drills into AP essentials: crafting and supporting arguments (Claims and Evidence), logical structuring (Reasoning and Organization), the art of persuasion (Rhetorical Style), and forming arguments grounded in text analysis (Developing textually substantiated arguments). It's a weekly workout for the mind, prepping students for in-depth discussions with less prep and time.

Remember that the true treasure of the Claim Jumper Edu-Protocol is empowering our students to become critical thinkers and articulate communicators. By guiding them through this activity with multiple iterations of increasing difficulty, we're not just teaching them to analyze text; we're equipping them with the skills to navigate the complex terrain of ideas and arguments they'll encounter throughout their lives.

Chapter 9
Walk the Line EduProtocol

The fourth-century philosopher Aristotle once proposed that the whole is greater than the sum of its parts. This idea, while resonant on a philosophical level, tends to crumble under the scrutiny of rhetorical analysis. Here, details matter; an argument is only as strong as its weakest link. Each component of rhetoric—each claim, each piece of evidence—serves as a crucial pillar. Should one falter, the entire structure may fall.

In the Walk the Line EduProtocol, students dissect a text's reasoning by examining its evidentiary claims and rhetorical choices, constructing a detailed blueprint of the argument. This practice illuminates the argument's framework, spotlighting its strengths and exposing any cracks in its foundation. By applying the *truth condition* (ensuring each claim is factually accurate) and the *logic condition* (assessing if the claims cohesively lead to the conclusion), the argument's overall integrity is revealed.

Developing these analytical skills is essential for students, equipping them to navigate an increasingly complex world filled with persuasive language and arguments. This EduProtocol sets students up for success by breaking down the process into discernible steps. It teaches them to critically evaluate what they read and hear, to look beyond face value, and to build cogent arguments of their own. In essence, it prepares them to be not just consumers of information but judicious analysts of it.

Walk the Line

 LOGIC

 CLAIMS

 CONDITIONS

 ANALYSIS

Academic Goals

Through successful implementation of Walk the Line, students should be able to:

- Distill a text's line of reasoning into its component parts
- Recognize and evaluate the claims and thesis in a piece of rhetoric
- Recognize and interpret evidence
- Recognize rhetorical choices and relate those choices to the effectiveness of a text's overall argument
- Examine the conditions of truth and logic in an argument
- Judge the efficacy of an argument based on truth and logic conditions
- Defend their analysis of a rhetorical resource

Marlena

This critical thinking skill, while obviously necessary, is often challenging to develop. Walk the Line provides a pathway forward. No pun intended!

Teacher Big Ideas

- By examining the line of reasoning of a rhetorical resource, students can verify the soundness of an argument and therefore analyze its effectiveness based on the internal structure of the argument itself.
- Work done in Walk the Line translates to other EduProtocols. Elements uncovered in this activity (logic, claims, theses, etc.) can enable further examination with, among others, Claim Jumper and "We Have a Situation Here!"
- In partnership with "We Have a Situation Here!" and Claim Jumper, this EduProtocol builds a robust scaffold for a defensible written analysis of a resource.

Jake

How about a template deck?

Prepare for the Activity

1. Ensure that students understand the conditions of classical logic: truth, logic, and soundness. To review:

- ▶ Truth: All claims must be factually correct. Each claim is described as either factually correct or factually incorrect.
- ▶ Logic: The claims must lead logically to the conclusion. Each claim is described as valid or invalid.
- ▶ Soundness: If both conditions are met, the argument is sound. If one or more conditions are not met, the argument is unsound.

2. Ensure that students understand the function of claims in an argument, meaning how they support the overarching thesis with evidence.

3. Ensure that students can recognize rhetorical choices, or ensure that you provide students with the necessary context for their analysis.

4. Link a rhetorical resource (reading selection, video, audio, comic, piece of artwork, etc.) to the assignment resource slide.

5. Decide if you want the students to present the argument in standard form logic, a method of structuring arguments where each claim or premise is presented as a distinct, numbered statement, leading logically to a conclusion. This format helps in identifying the structure and validity of arguments by laying them out in a clear, sequential order. Then, select your appropriate slide for the task.

6. If you're running Walk the Line digitally, prepare a template deck for students to use. Ensure that there are several claim slides for the students to work on or instruct students to copy enough for their needs.

7. If you're running Walk the Line with a print resource, design an example and determine how students will research the background.

8. Assign your Walk the Line activity to students.

Jake

Here's an example of standard form logic:

Premise: All mammals need oxygen to survive.

Premise: Dolphins are mammals.

Conclusion: Therefore, dolphins need oxygen to survive.

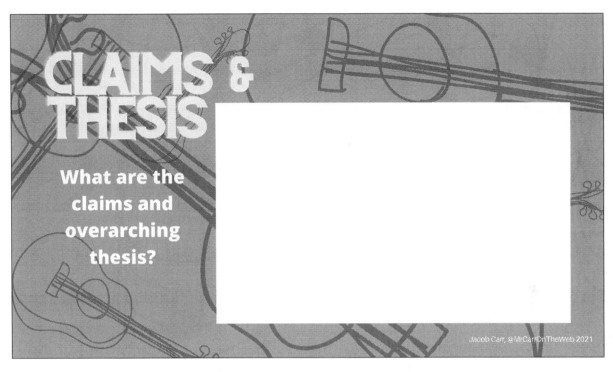

Instructions

1. Begin by first familiarizing the class with a selection of rhetoric. You might choose to complete prereading activities, annotations, class discussion, or otherwise. Then, depending on the class's skill, direct students to complete analyses of that text in small groups or individually.

2. Students start by breaking down the text into its individual claims and identifying the central thesis. Then, guide them to present this information in a clear, organized manner. They can use bullet points for simplicity or structure their findings in standard form logic, where arguments are laid out in a precise, numbered format. This way, each premise leads logically to the conclusion, making it easier to follow and evaluate the argument's flow. Adapt the slides to facilitate whichever method best suits the lesson's objectives.

3. Once students understand the text's individual claims and thesis, they should divide those claims among team members or work with each claim individually, pulling out

evidence from the resource and recognizing the rhetorical choices used to develop each claim. Students should repeat this step as often as necessary for the assignment.

4. After examining the individual claims, students should apply the conditions of truth and logic. Then, working as a group, teams present the requirements before discussing the overall soundness of the text's argument.

5. After interpreting the conditions of the argument, direct students to construct an analysis showing how each claim leads to the thesis and how the construction of the text creates cohesion and unity in the argument. This should lead finally to a discussion of the overall efficacy of the argument. Depending on your goals, you may require this discussion to take the form of a written paragraph describing elements in significant concepts, a group presentation of individual facets of the argument, or even a lengthy, in-depth analysis that presents evidence in a formal writing project.

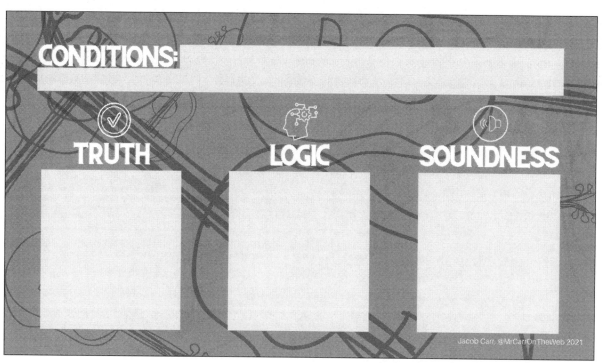

Helping students analyze an argument based on the laws of truth and logic helps them understand whether or not an argument is sound.

Key Points to Remember

- This activity is not meant to be a first step in rhetorical analysis. Instead, ensure students are equipped with the skills required to analyze rhetoric before jumping into Walk the Line. To develop these skills, utilize Skill Builder activities, Claim Jumper, and other EduProtocols first.

- Begin with straightforward and brief texts to develop students' analytical skills before tackling complex rhetoric in the Walk the Line EduProtocol. Start with simple resources like commercials, ads, short-form videos (e.g., TikTok, Instagram, YouTube Shorts), comics, and other basic materials. This approach helps students focus on the task without being overwhelmed. As they become more adept and the cognitive load lessens, gradually introduce more and more challenging material to increase their ability.

Variations

Whole Group

Work through Steps 2 to 4 of this EduProtocol. Have students individually write their paragraphs and share them with the class. Consider using Thick Slides, Socrative, or a similar shared platform. This will help build collaboration.

Nacho Analysis

In this variation using the Nacho Paragraph EduProtocol, once individual analysis paragraphs are submitted, the class will select one that either needs further development or showcases exceptional analysis. The class then applies the Nacho Paragraph approach, which is a collaborative editing and enhancement technique. The entire class collectively refines this chosen paragraph, with each student proposing improvements to strengthen the line of reasoning and suggest robust support for the claims. The Nacho Paragraph method turns a single student's work into a product of

Feed a GPT model the rubric and five or six examples of student analysis paragraphs spanning varying abilities. Have it return feedback that works for all the samples. Pass this on to students.

collective intelligence, where everyone adds their flavor to enhance the substance and style of the analysis, ensuring the argument is not only clear and well presented but also logically sound and convincingly argued. This can be done as a whole class together or individually.

Peer Review

Use Walk the Line to look at arguments crafted by students as part of their writing process. For example, the resource material could be a detailed outline composed by a student with claims and evidence. For the "rhetorical choices" aspect, the reviewing student could offer suggestions for improving the writing, focusing on enhancing what is already written.

Modification for Middle Grades

- Provide a finished piece of writing for this EduProtocol with claims, evidence, and rhetorical choices. Have the students determine the conditions and provide an analysis.
- Provide the thesis and claims for the students to work with.
- Predetermine the rhetorical choices students should look for, and have students extract them from the material.

AP Adaptation and Correlation to Enduring Understandings

Walk the Line is an AP/College Board heavy hitter. It functions well at a lower level, with the heavier scaffolding a freshman English class might need. But it truly shines when students are willing to analyze and think deeply about the construction of a text. With caution, and once students begin to grasp the concepts firmly, move them away from using this EduProtocol as a group and toward using it individually. This will help foster deeply individualized thinking, which will serve them well not only on the AP Exam but also further along in their educational journey and beyond.

(1) RHETORICAL APPEALS

(2) STASIS

(3) CHOICES

(4) PRÉCIS

In *My First Summer in the Sierra*, the acclaimed naturalist John Muir wrote, **"When we try to pick out anything by itself, we find it hitched to everything else in the Universe."** As with the natural world, nothing in communication stands alone; communication always links us to the world around us. When we place a piece of rhetoric into the environment from which it originated, we learn much about its purpose, drive, and effects.

"We Have a Situation Here!" (WHASH) is an EduProtocol that helps students examine a resource in situ. By looking at a source's creator, its recipients, its reason for existence, and other aspects referred to as the *rhetorical situation*, we understand the piece's life and how it altered the topic's discourse.

Through this EduProtocol, students write a detailed rhetorical summary or précis that lays out the resource's argument, intentions, choices, and intended audience. By understanding this as a foundation of the resource, students are better prepared to grasp the argument and its impact. If this process begins to feel like a history lesson or a dive into civics, you're likely on the right path!

Academic Goals

Through successful implementation of "We Have a Situation Here!," students should be able to:

Jon

WHASH is all about the EduProtocols mindset. Things are connected instead of being in silos. Teaching isolated topics is great for practice, but at some point, you've got to be able to execute on the big picture.

- Identify and describe the rhetorical situation of a text or resource
- Interpret the effects of the rhetorical situation in terms of speaker, audience, exigence, purpose, message, and choices
- Connect the rhetorical situation's effect to the argument itself
- Assess the gap between the author's stance and the intended audience's perspective on the argument to determine the necessary development of ethos within the rhetorical situation
- Reframe elements of the rhetorical situation in the form of a rhetorical précis, a structured four-sentence paragraph that succinctly summarizes the text's central argument, evidence, and purpose while also describing the intended audience's response
- Identify the author's overarching rhetorical choices and techniques and develop ideas on how these function within the argument
- Appraise the author's choices, their effectiveness, and how they interplay with the situation itself

Teacher Big Ideas

- Work done in WHASH translates to other EduProtocols. For example, elements uncovered in this activity (claims, theses, etc.) enable a further examination with Claim Jumper, Walk the Line, and other EduProtocols. WHASH also puts into practice individual skills gained in 8 p*ARTS, Fast and Curious, and other prior foundational content.
- Don't rush the process of introducing students to the historical context of the resource, author, and background information. Instead, provide adequate resources and direction for students to interact with the material. Con-

sider audio and video speeches, biographies, news articles, essays, etc., as primary resources. Utilizing items like interviews with the author, documentaries on the historical period, history textbooks, interactive timelines, and cultural analyses can help situate the resource within its historical and cultural setting. This approach will give students a deeper understanding of the rhetorical situation and allow them to gain a more profound knowledge of the text's context and significance.

- Systematically moving through the rhetorical situation slide by slide will help students not to feel overwhelmed by the process.

- By deconstructing and examining the rhetorical situation of a given resource, its relationship to the author's intent, and the execution of an argument, students will begin to consider how others may receive their work.

- In partnership with Walk the Line and Claim Jumper, this protocol builds a robust scaffold that leads toward a defensible written resource analysis.

Prepare for the Activity

1. Link a rhetorical resource (reading selection, video, audio, comic, piece of artwork, etc.) to the assignment resource slide.

2. Provide other linked materials to help students learn about the author, when and where the resource was published, the cultural elements surrounding it, etc.

3. If running WHASH digitally, prepare a template deck for students to use. If you implement the EduProtocol with physical materials, design an example and determine how students will research the background.

4. If you use a specific template for a rhetorical précis, link it to the rhetorical précis slide.

5. Distribute the assignment to students.

Jake

How about a template deck?

Instructions

1. Begin by introducing the background and cultural history of the resource. This involves exploring the societal, political, and artistic influences of the time and place in which the resource was created. Discuss aspects like prevailing societal norms, historical events, and prevalent artistic trends that may have influenced the resource.

2. Decide on your teaching approach:
   - ▶ Teacher-led: You can choose to present this information directly, providing a comprehensive and curated overview to the students.
   - ▶ Student-centered: Alternatively, encourage students to engage in independent research. Guide them to gather and share various materials such as videos, audio clips, images, and primary source documents. This can be done in addition to the resources you provide.

3. Whether you choose a teacher- or student-led approach, the goal is to foster a deep understanding of the resource's context. This includes exploring the time period, the author's background, the target audience at the time, and the cultural landscape. Ensure students grasp the context in which the resource was produced and its intended purpose. Prioritize a thorough exploration of a few well-chosen sources over a quick overview of many.

4. Once students understand the resource elements in context, they can begin interacting with the primary rhetorical resource, such as a speech, article, etc. As they start understanding the structure of the resource, they also sort the material and fill out the information via the WHASH deck.
   - ▶ Ethos
     - ◆ Who is the speaker?

- ◆ How are they qualified to present the information covered in the text?
- ◆ How did they address their audience?
- ▶ Pathos
  - ◆ Who is the audience?
  - ◆ How do they feel about the speaker?
  - ◆ How likely are they to agree with the text's argument?
- ▶ Kairos
  - ◆ When and where was the material presented?
  - ◆ How does this cultural context affect the argument?
  - ◆ How urgent is the message?
- ▶ Logos
  - ◆ What is the controlling thesis?
  - ◆ How does the thesis relate to the audience?
  - ◆ What claims does the argument pursue?
- ▶ Stasis
  - ◆ What are the extremes of the position?
  - ◆ Where on the line does the speaker fall?
  - ◆ Where on the line is their audience?
  - ◆ What can we infer from the distance between the speaker and the audience?

5. Once students understand the rhetorical situation, engage the group in analyzing the stasis theory. Evaluate the gap between the author's perspective and the audience's viewpoint, as well as where the text's stance falls within the broader spectrum of discourse on the topic. This process helps students identify and assess the urgency and significance of the argument. For instance, contrast the different impacts of a political figure addressing their supporters at a rally versus an activist presenting their case in an adversarial courtroom.

6. Finally, students use what they've developed to create a rhetorical précis. While there are many ways of doing this, here's one that I find works well.

Introduction Sentence:

- Start with the author's name, the genre and title of the work, the date of publication in parentheses, a rhetorically accurate verb (such as *asserts*, *argues*, *refutes*, *proves*, *explains*, etc.), and a clause containing the thesis statement of the work.

- Example: [Author's Name], in the [genre] "[Title]" (Date), argues that [thesis statement].

An Account of the Argument:

- Describe how the author supports the thesis statement, outlining the key elements of the argument and the methods or approaches used.

- Example: [He/She/They] supports this argument by [explaining/illustrating/defining/etc.] [key points of support], using [methods/approaches such as surveys, case studies, statistical analysis, logical reasoning, anecdotes, etc.].

Statement of the Author's Purpose:

- Explain the author's intended effect on the audience and why the author wrote the text. Often, the author's own words are included in this step.

- Example: [The author's] purpose is to [what the author does in the text, e.g., challenge, raise awareness, criticize, defend] in order to [what the author wants to accomplish with the audience, e.g., convince readers of something, demonstrate the importance of something, persuade audiences to consider something].

Description of the Intended Audience and the Relationship the Author Establishes:

- Identify the author's intended audience and the relationship the author establishes with them, as well as the social or cultural context the author is writing in.

- Example: [He/She] establishes a [relationship type, e.g., formal, informal, professional, personal] relationship with [his/her] intended audience of [identify the audience, e.g., students, professionals, young adults, etc.], suggesting that [mention any insights into the relationship or context that are relevant to the argument].

Here's a Completed Example:

Martin Luther King Jr.'s "Letter from Birmingham Jail" was written in 1963 after his arrest for participating in a nonviolent protest against segregation. In the letter, King indeed addresses criticism from white Southern clergymen who had denounced the protests as "unwise and untimely" and branded him an "outsider." King

Jake

Understanding the range of the argument is crucial to understanding the rhetorical situation. For example, if the argument were that students should typically not have cell phones in class, the range would be from "always" to "never," with the author falling somewhere nearer the "never" side. In contrast, the audience would likely fall nearer the "always" side if they were students. This gap represents how much of a burden of proof lies with the author.

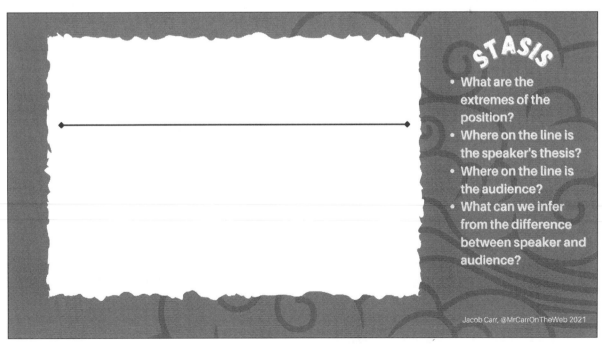

Here, students are plotting just how far apart different stakeholders are in regards to their beliefs in an argument.

articulates the steps of any nonviolent campaign as fact-finding, negotiation, self-purification, and direct action. He also makes a distinction between just and unjust laws, stating that individuals have a moral duty to follow just laws while having an obligation to disobey unjust laws, which he defines as any law that degrades human personality or is imposed on a minority that had no part in enacting or creating the law.

Key Points to Remember

- This protocol asks a lot of students and needs to be scaffolded early and densely. Consider beginning with Edu-Protocols that introduce and practice the individual elements of the rhetorical situation and choices.

- Spending time building students' competencies around rhetorical choices will significantly help them to navigate this EduProtocol. Consider providing a sample list of frequently used options.

- Consider finding materials that reflect students as individuals or draw upon their interests. While this aids engagement, it can also be overwhelming initially. If you direct students to find their own reference and background material, do so with caution, ensuring that there will be enough readily available historical and cultural material. The key part of this EduProtocol is uncovering why the elements of the rhetorical situation are important, not the research methodology and process behind finding the material. Without proper background information, a rhetorical situation becomes uninteresting and unmeaningful.

Variations

Whole-to-Part Grouping

1. Like in the baseline EduProtocol, follow the first steps to build background information around a single topic or historical event as a class.
2. Then, divide the class into groups to work on a set of rhetorical resources pertaining to that event.

Here are some options:

- Option 1: Divide the class into groups. Give each group a resource to analyze that fits within the historical event previously discussed.
- Option 2: Choose four to five resources for the class. Give each group member a different resource, but give each group moments to collaborate with other groups. This is a simple way to differentiate the difficulty of the resource.

Here are some possible sets based on single events:

- The civil rights movement:
  - ▶ Martin Luther King Jr.'s "I Have a Dream"
  - ▶ Malcolm X's "The Ballot or the Bullet"
  - ▶ John F. Kennedy's civil rights address
  - ▶ Lyndon B. Johnson's "We Shall Overcome"
  - ▶ Robert F. Kennedy's speech on the assassination of Martin Luther King Jr.
- The women's suffrage movement:
  - ▶ Susan B. Anthony's "On Women's Right to Vote"
  - ▶ Sojourner Truth's "Ain't I a Woman?"
  - ▶ Elizabeth Cady Stanton's "Solitude of Self"
  - ▶ Carrie Chapman Catt's "The Crisis"
  - ▶ Emmeline Pankhurst's "Freedom or Death"
- World War II and its aftermath:
  - ▶ Winston Churchill's "We Shall Fight on the Beaches"

Ask AI to explain the historical events surrounding a piece of rhetoric. You can even have it rewrite the information into a simple story for students to interact with to understand the provenance better.

- ▶ Franklin D. Roosevelt's "A Date Which Will Live in Infamy"
- ▶ Charles de Gaulle's "Appeal of 18 June"
- ▶ Harry S. Truman's announcement of the dropping of the atomic bomb
- ▶ Winston Churchill's "Iron Curtain"
- The end of apartheid in South Africa:
  - ▶ Nelson Mandela's "I Am Prepared to Die" speech at Rivonia Trial
  - ▶ F. W. de Klerk's speech announcing the repeal of apartheid laws
  - ▶ Nelson Mandela's presidential inauguration speech
  - ▶ Desmond Tutu's "Rainbow Nation"
  - ▶ Thabo Mbeki's "I Am an African"
- The fall of the Berlin Wall and the end of the Cold War:
  - ▶ Ronald Reagan's "Tear Down This Wall"
  - ▶ Mikhail Gorbachev's speech at the United Nations
  - ▶ George H. W. Bush's "A Europe Whole and Free"
  - ▶ Helmut Kohl's speech on German reunification
  - ▶ Václav Havel's address to the US Congress
- In the end, have students with the same resource present their findings to the class. After the groups have offered their analyses, discuss how each resource enlightens their understanding of the event, enhancing understanding of the rhetorical situation.

Single Combat!

1. Find a topic of study for the whole class, such as a historical event, a current media focus, or debatable issues. Then, similar to the whole-group variation, work together as a class to build background information, trying to find as neutral a position as possible.

2. Next, find rhetorical pieces which contradict and argue against one another. Groups or individuals should work

through their single rhetorical resources with the WHASH protocol and present their information to the class. This is an excellent opportunity for students to explore opinions that don't align with their own. As they learn to clinically dissect an argument and present their précis to the class, an even greater whole picture of the event will be formed.

3. After presentations, discuss any changes of opinion or alterations of understanding the students made during the process.

The Practicum

Once students are proficient with this EduProtocol, set them loose. Have students find their own topics, background information, and rhetorical resources to study. Consider a gallery assignment where students present their findings.

Modification for Middle Grades Whole Group

1. Choose a single resource and work through it as a group to introduce the WHASH. You could begin this process with a Group Brainstorm EduProtocol (see book 1 of *The Edu-Protocol Field Guide*), whereby students collectively offer topics to be studied. Next, through a process of elimination, lead the class to a single issue. Then, as the teacher, find a relevant primary resource and background information to provide them with a curated file from which to draw.

2. To understand the background information, have students self-select from the historical information provided. Be sure to have an array of audio, visual, print, digital, and other forms of media. Then, together as a class, build the milieu of the resource before looking at the resource itself. For example, let's say you were reading a speech from Rep. Shirley Chisholm at Howard University on April

21, 1969. You could offer resources about the protests on campus the previous year, the climate for African American university students in the United States at the time, the Vietnam War–era climate in the eastern United States and at universities across the country, the assassination of Martin Luther King Jr., the Voting Rights Act of 1965, a biography of Rep. Shirley Chisolm, and many other materials to contextualize the environment in which she gave her speech.

3. After understanding the background, move as a class through the speech, annotate important passages, look for rhetorical choices, and pull out the overarching thesis and claims presented.

4. Finally, consider reflecting on each slide as a group before moving on to the next. Making sure students understand your expectations will help ensure that they'll be even more successful the next time they do the protocol.

AP Adaptation and Correlation to Enduring Understandings

For the AP Exam, students need to understand rhetorical abstraction. Using WHASH to analyze a text's rhetorical situation and argument structure helps them grasp the core of rhetoric. This aligns with AP's Enduring Understandings: recognizing rhetorical situations, appreciating styles, and constructing solid arguments about a text's meaning. Regular practice with various rhetorical forms enhances students' analytical and argumentative skills.

(1) TRAIN

(2) PROTECT

(3) CONSTRUCT

(4) BATTLE

Based on the old-fashioned "Who would win in a battle?" game, Unto the Breach is a game-based EduProtocol for exploring and developing claims in a fun, low-stakes way. By creatively using emojis to build a character, with all their battle strengths and weaknesses, students playfully move through the development of an argument and practice writing strong introductions. After getting used to putting together an argument for fun, students will be better equipped to develop arguments—with supporting claims—in formal assignments.

Academic Goals

Through successful implementation of Unto the Breach, students should be able to:

- Craft claims and counterarguments that they can support with evidence

- Write concession-thesis-reason introductory paragraphs that preview the structure of an overall argument and that include background knowledge and counterarguments

- Provide feedback to the author of an argument based on their line of reasoning and support for the overarching thesis

Jake

How about a template deck?

Marlena

If they can say it, they can write it!

Jake

You want a printable graphic organizer for this one? Sure, I've got that!

Emily

This is a great way to gain experience in argumentation. Since students are raising arguments and defending their own in the classroom, they must quickly think on their feet and develop strong arguments. Exercises like this helped me to build the skills I needed to write a strong essay later.

Teacher Big Ideas

- This activity is meant to be fun and creative. Celebrate out-of-the-box thinking.

- Introduce Unto the Breach without the written portions. Just pull up the emojis, let students assign them as heroes/strengths/weaknesses, and host quick verbal debates over who would win. This could be done as a whole class with students forming loose paragraphs about their heroes and posting them to Socrative for a class-wide vote.

- As students gain confidence, up the ante by introducing the research and writing portions of Unto the Breach.

Prepare for the Activity

1. Decide whether the activity would better serve students with a graphic organizer (printed) or the artistic slide deck (digital).

2. Assign either the graphic organizer or slide deck to the class.

3. Familiarize yourself with the Random Emoji Generator on the EduProtocols website. The emojis can be selected before the class period and handed out or selected in real time as a class.

Instructions

1. Divide the class into two large groups. In groups, students will have the opportunity to think more creatively about emojis.

2. Select five emojis for each large group using the Random Emoji Generator, which is available at eduprotocols.com/class.

Students organize their strengths and weaknesses graphically

3. Direct students to look at their emojis and assign one to be their hero, three to be strengths/armaments for their hero, and one to be their hero's weakness.

4. Working on either their graphic organizer or slide deck, students begin to defend their strengths with a resource/ citation. For example, if a student assigned a sushi emoji as one of their hero's strengths, they could write, "Ability to deftly wield a chef's knife" or "Deadly skilled with chopsticks" as their strength. They might even get extra creative and say, "Able to conjure and deploy boiling water." They then find some real-world citation that explains why that would be beneficial as a weapon/skill. For example, maybe they cite the temperature of boiling water and the damage it could cause, an example of chopsticks being used as weapons, or a historical example where a chef defended their restaurant.

5. After developing their skills, students tackle their weaknesses. The point of identifying a weakness is to divulge

what their opponent would attack as a shortcoming but show that it is, in fact, a strength. For example, perhaps one group's emoji is a Ferris wheel, and they decide their weakness is "Afraid of carnies." Then, students would construct a concession statement such as "While X may be afraid of carnies, they have developed this fear into an acute awareness of people around them, which in turn becomes a strength of preemptively seeing danger coming their way."

Construct Your Argument

Now, put it all together. Write the introduction to an argument by stacking a hook, background information, consession-thesis-reason statement, and claims.

As a final element, students put the whole thing together in the form of an introductory paragraph for a persuasive essay.

6. Next, students construct an introduction that describes their hero. They need a hook, background information, and a concession-thesis-reason statement.

Here's an extended example:

- **Emojis:** mailbox (hero); needle, train, nurse hat (strengths); Ferris wheel (weakness)

- ♦ **Introduction paragraph:** "Do you dare put the motto of the US Postal Service to the test? 'Neither snow nor rain nor heat nor gloom of night' will stop Roger the Mailman from winning in battle. Hailing from the suburban wilds of Durham, California, this public servant knows a thing or two about danger. While some may say that a fear of carnies is a weakness, Roger has developed this fear into an acute awareness of people around him, which in turn became a strength of preemptively seeing danger coming his way. This awareness, paired with the ability to throw poison-tipped needles accurately, the speed of a bullet train, and his rapid-healing power all combine to make Roger a super-threat in the realm of battle."

7. Once the introduction is written, assign groups of four to six students to form battle groups.

8. The battle group decides on two people to face off. The debate moves as follows:

    ► Round 1: Each opponent reads their introduction.

    ► Round 2: Opponents raise arguments in a back-and-forth manner that explains why their strengths would win based on their researched claims.

    ► When the argument wanes, the audience discusses the efficacy of each line of reasoning based on claims and reflects their findings to the authors. Based on these reflections, the winner is chosen.

9. The winner battles the next opponent, and so on until there is a winner.

10. [Optional] Table winners do battle for a class-wide winner.

Key Points to Remember

- This activity is a time for flexible creativity.
- Once students complete Unto the Breach a few times with the outline, they become very quick at constructing their arguments. Multiple repetitions of this EduProtocol lead to solid constructions of valid arguments.

Variations

Let students plug in their characters and have AI generate a story for their background.

Skirmish

- For this variation, skip the step of backing claims with resources. This variation is just about flexible thinking and constructing fictitious arguments.
- Once introductions are written, students post them to Socrative or a shared slide deck instead of hosting a verbal debate. Students then read and vote on which hero they think would win in an all-out battle based on these criteria:
  - ▶ Is the paragraph complete?
  - ▶ Are the emojis used creatively?
- Unto the Breach could also be completed by verbalizing, reading, and voting in smaller groups as a bracket system.
- This version is meant to be quick and silly, leading to more in-depth treatments later.

All-Out War

Complete the activity as previously intended, but create a class-wide tournament bracket instead of table groups. Again, there are many online generators to assist with this.

Pit Crew

When a player is defeated, they join the team of the winner. The winner's team can swap out an attribute from the defeated player. For example, they can swap out either a strength or a weakness. The pit crew has a few minutes to rework their argument before entering the next battle.

Superfight Card Game

Jack Dire (Skybound) created a fantastic card game called Superfight: A Card Game of Absurd Arguments, which inspired this EduProtocol. I use this card game multiple times per year. Consider supporting Jack Dire by purchasing the game and using it in your implementation of Unto the Breach. Replace emojis with Superfight cards, but play according to Unto the Breach rules.

Writing Extension

Once students have a good introduction, allow them time to write their arguments as complete essays, bringing in more sources and citations to back each claim.

Reverse Engineering

- In this variation, the process is inverted. Begin by providing students with a prewritten argument or story about a fictional hero, complete with strengths, weaknesses, and a background narrative. However, the emojis representing these elements are not disclosed.

- The task for the students is to analyze the text and deduce which emojis could represent the hero, their strengths, and their weaknesses. This encourages critical thinking and analytical skills, as students need to infer and match the textual descriptions with appropriate emojis.

- After the students make their choices, have them share them with the class. This allows for a comparison between students' interpretations, fostering a discussion about

Using a GPT model is a simple way to create a whole set of stories for this variation! Just give it a prompt like "Create a short story about a fictional hero." The hero should have distinct strengths and weaknesses as well as a unique background. However, do not explicitly mention these attributes. Instead, describe them in a way that hints at specific emojis that could represent these traits. The story should be engaging and leave room for interpretation, allowing students to guess which emojis best fit the hero's characteristics. The narrative should be suitable for middle or high school students and should be about two hundred words long.

how different symbols (emojis) can convey similar ideas or characteristics.

- This reverse engineering approach can be particularly engaging, as it challenges students to think backward from the finished product to the foundational elements, offering a unique perspective on constructing arguments and narratives.

Content Argument!

Instead of emojis, students take attributes from content-specific items from another class and form an argument about their heroes using the structure of Unto the Breach (hook, background, concession, claims). This works well when presented as a Thick Slide.

Example: Think your muscles and brain are the most important parts of your body? Think again! It turns out the real MVPs are actually tiny little powerhouses called mitochondria. They may be small, but they're essential for everything you do, from thinking to breathing to even singing karaoke. So the next time you're feeling tired, remember to thank your mitochondria for working hard to keep you going!

AP Adaptation and Correlation to Enduring Understandings

Unto the Breach transforms the learning of rhetorical presentation into a stress-free, enjoyable experience by gamifying the process, which is particularly beneficial in high-pressure environments like AP courses. This approach helps to alleviate the students' fight-or-flight response, fostering a relaxed and playful atmosphere that encourages laughter and whimsy. Engaging in this fun, game-like setting not only makes students comfortable but also deepens their understanding of key elements such as the rhetorical situation, claims and evidence, reasoning and organization, and the nuanced roles of word choice, imagery, and symbols in crafting persuasive, textually substantiated arguments. Don't underestimate the power of this playful method—it's an effective and insightful way to learn.

Self-reflection is essential for education because it helps students to examine their ideas, feelings, emotions, and behaviors. When students can objectively look at themselves, they learn about their successes and progress. Through self-reflection, students also become more aware of the practices that are effective for them.

Based loosely on the work of John Hattie, Yes-Phew-Made-It-Grew! (YPMG!) provides a predictable space for students to reflect, both as a predictive and summative activity. By looking forward to the growth required to succeed at a given task, students can set goals and plan for success. And by looking at what they've done, they can recognize their strengths and celebrate the achievements they made.

Academic Goals

Through successful implementation of Yes-Phew-Made-It!-Grew!, students should be able to:

- Reflect on their learning process
- Celebrate their success
- Recognize their growth

Marlena

John Hattie found that self-efficacy has a big impact, with an effect size of .92. One effective way to boost student confidence and efficacy is through the cycle of reflection and goal-setting to understand how effort leads to rewards and a sense of pride in their achievements.

After completing their YPMG!, have students plug their reflections into a GPT model. Ask it to return a script for a short-form video of less than sixty seconds. As an extension, have students create these videos.

Jake

How about a template deck?

Teacher Big Ideas

- Because YPMG! is based on a version of the classic Frayer Model, students should be able to adapt to it with very little how-to instruction, allowing frequent repetition.
- This activity can be a simple entry/exit ticket strategy for formative assessment.
- YPMG! is scalable to fit any point in the process of completing an assignment. It's usable as a check-in for a single activity or even the whole year!

Prepare for the Activity

1. Make a copy of the template deck so you always have it. You could also recreate this by making a typical four-quadrant graphic organizer. Each quadrant contains one of the YPMG! aspects (yes, phew, made it, grew).

2. Edit the topic for review on slide 1.

3. Make enough copies of the student slide for everyone in your class. Then, everyone should work in the same deck in order to read each other's answers.

4. If you have multiple classes or sections, consider making a slide with the class designation. Then have enough slides for all students! Students will need to drag their finished slide under the proper class time. You learn this organization tactic once, then all your data is in one place, and you can see what's happening in other sections.

5. Change sharing permissions so every student can edit this deck.

6. When the deck is complete, delete the instructions slide and assign it.

7. This activity also works well printed.

[Student's name]   **YPMG!**

YES!	PHEW!!!

MADE IT!!!	GREW!!

Instructions

1. Students should pick a slide and put their names on it.

2. Through the course of reflection, students should answer the following prompts in just two to three sentences each; they shouldn't overdo it. Tell students that they should consider adding an emoji to each prompt, too:

   ▶ YES! What is something about this assignment that you thought you'd enjoy—and you did?

   ▶ PHEW! What is something about this assignment that you weren't looking forward to but that turned out OK?

   ▶ MADE IT! What is something about this assignment you thought would be difficult, and it was?

   ▶ GREW! What is the one skill you feel you grew in the most over the course of this assignment or activity?

3. Once complete, students should move their slides to the top of the deck (just below the directions slide). This action helps keep things organized.

The use of reflection in an AP setting is crucial to learning and development. Self-reflection helps a student determine not only their points of need but, importantly, their strengths. By building a balanced understanding of their knowledge and skills, students gain the confidence to work toward higher achievement.

Key Points to Remember

- This activity shouldn't be a graded assignment but a tool for awareness. If extrinsic motivation is required, consider grading only for completion.
- Having multiple students' reflections in one deck allows for collaboration. When students see that other students struggle or need to learn the same things, that makes them less anxious about their learning process.

AP Adaptation and Correlation to Enduring Understandings

YPMG! can support any Enduring Understanding, depending on how you utilize it.

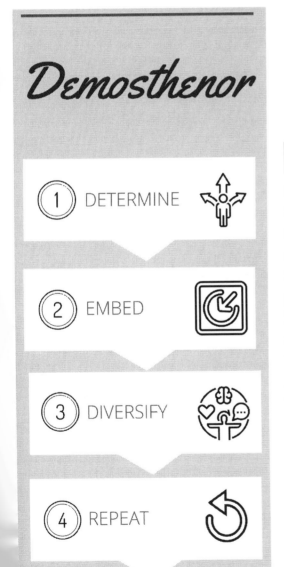

Demosthenor

1. DETERMINE
2. EMBED
3. DIVERSIFY
4. REPEAT

We don't make the products you buy.
We make the products you buy better.

—1990s BASF Ad Campaign

Hailed as one of the greatest orators of ancient Greece, Demosthenes was recorded as, for all his talents as a speaker, one who worked purposefully on his craft. Anecdotal stories abound of him speaking with pebbles in his mouth to overcome a speech impediment, speaking loudly enough to be heard over the waves at a beach, and even constructing an underground practice space to focus uninterruptedly on his work. As such, Demosthenes is an example of how working hard on specific skills to get better at something complex can yield great results. He didn't just speak repeatedly; he broke his weaknesses into manageable chunks and overcame them purposefully. Inspired by his legacy, the Demosthenor Toolkit—a creative blend of Demosthenes's name with the suffix -or, denoting a practitioner or mentor—embodies this systematic approach to mastering the art of oration. It is designed to mentor students in the same detailed, deliberate manner, transforming them into articulate speakers ready to captivate any audience.

The Demosthenor EduProtocol helps students with public speaking. It is designed to be completed frequently in smaller chunks and used in conjunction with other EduProtocols or, less often, as a whole scaffold. Either way, the EduProtocol focuses on training students to organize their thoughts into words, understand how their message will likely be received, and deliver those words to an audience.

Like the BASF campaign, the true beauty of the Demosthenor EduProtocol isn't that it results in a speech similar to a TED talk. Although it *could* yield that outcome, it's about improving other activities. Students must hone each compounded skill for it to happen fluidly. Still, when we break public speaking down into manageable pieces, students can work on that skill like Demosthenes. And work they must, for as Hesiod, another Greek, put it, "Before the gates of excellence the high gods have placed sweat."

Academic Goals

Through successful implementation of the Demosthenor EduProtocol, students should be able to:

- Isolate and practice the individual skills required for public speaking
- Provide a repeatable scaffold for public speaking that is scalable from a few moments to lengthy orations

Teacher Big Ideas

- Utilizing individual elements of the Demosthenor EduProtocol heightens the experience of other activities and EduProtocols by adding elements of public speaking.
- The Demosthenor EduProtocol can be seen as a set of ingredients. You can practice each individually, mix together several, or even construct a full-fledged speaking project using its pieces.

Jake

The Demosthenor Edu-Protocol is unlike anything else in the EduProtocols approach. Think of it as a menu of side dishes you add to the meal. Maybe you're doing an Iron Chef Lesson about Mesopotamia. You could drop in one of the Audience slides to help students identify who will receive their micropresentation.

Marlena

Every student will, at some point, need to sit through an interview and sell themselves as the ideal candidate, but many students lack public speaking and communication skills. How do they even start?

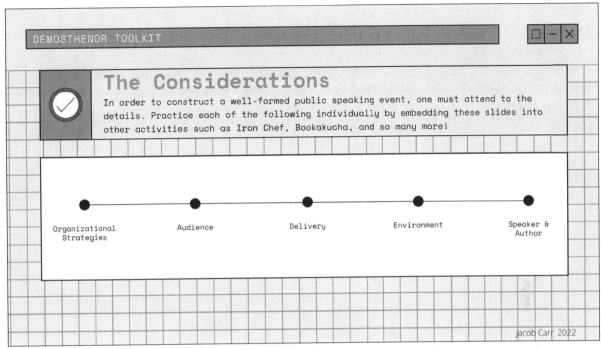

An overview of the five elements for public speaking

Prepare for the Activity

1. Review the Demosthenor skills.
2. Add one of those skills to an existing activity.

For example, if you're already completing a Walk the Line EduProtocol based on a speech, consider adding a Demosthenor Organizational Strategies slide where students format their analysis according to a specific purpose.

Or if you're completing a Frayer Model based on character traits, you could add a Demosthenor Delivery slide to prompt students to imagine the tools they could employ (props, volume, gestures, etc.) to convey their information to a given audience if asked to present their work.

Jake

How about a template deck?

Instructions

1. Determine which Demosthenor skill will be worked on.
2. Embed that skill into an existing assignment.
3. Repeat that skill frequently.

Organizational Skills

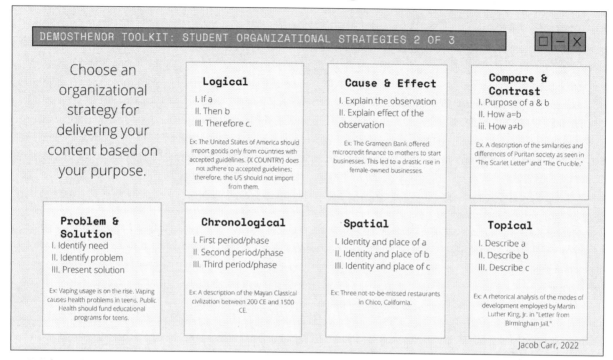

DEMOSTHENOR TOOLKIT: STUDENT ORGANIZATIONAL STRATEGIES 2 OF 3

Choose an organizational strategy for delivering your content based on your purpose.

Logical

I. If a
II. Then b
III. Therefore c.

Ex: The United States of America should import goods only from countries with accepted guidelines. {X COUNTRY} does not adhere to accepted guidelines; therefore, the US should not import from them.

Cause & Effect

I. Explain the observation
II. Explain effect of the observation

Ex: The Grameen Bank offered microcredit finance to mothers to start businesses. This led to a drastic rise in female-owned businesses.

Compare & Contrast

I. Purpose of a & b
II. How a=b
iii. How a≠b

Ex: A description of the similarities and differences of Puritan society as seen in "The Scarlet Letter" and "The Crucible."

Problem & Solution

I. Identify need
II. Identify problem
III. Present solution

Ex: Vaping usage is on the rise. Vaping causes health problems in teens. Public Health should fund educational programs for teens.

Chronological

I. First period/phase
II. Second period/phase
III. Third period/phase

Ex: A description of the Mayan Classical civilization between 200 CE and 1500 CE.

Spatial

I. Identity and place of a
II. Identity and place of b
III. Identity and place of c

Ex: Three not-to-be-missed restaurants in Chico, California.

Topical

I. Describe a
II. Describe b
III. Describe c

Ex: A rhetorical analysis of the modes of development employed by Martin Luther King, Jr. in "Letter from Birmingham Jail."

Jacob Carr, 2022

Students learn to self-select from various organizational strategies for the most effective delivery.

Let the students plug their information into a GPT along with a chosen strategy for the organization. Have AI return an outline reformatted according to the strategy! Students can then see personalized models of how to manipulate information.

"How will the material be structured?"

I've chosen seven strategies for organizing and presenting information based on the desired outcome. First, give students opportunities to choose which strategy best fits their purpose, then write an outline according to its structure.

7 WAYS TO ORGANIZE YOUR SPEECH/WRITING

-JAKE CARR, MR. CARR ON THE WEB

Jake

How about a printable poster of the organizational strategies?!

1. PERSUADE USING A LOGIC STRUCTURE

I. If a
II. Then b
III. Therefore c.

The United States should only import from countries with adequate regulations. X Country does not regulate, therefore, the United States should not import from X.

2. IDENTIFY A PROBLEM AND PRESENT A SOLUTION

I. Identify a need
II. Identify a problem
III. Present a solution

Vaping usage is on the rise. Vaping causes health problems in teens. Public health should fund education programs in schools.

3. DISCUSS AN OBSERVATION AND ITS OUTCOME

I. Explain the observation
II. Explain the effects of the observation

The Grameen Bank offered microcredit finance to mothers to start businesses. This led to a drastic rise in female-owned businesses.

4. PRESENT TIME-BASED INFORMATION

I. Early period
II. Middle period
III. Late period

The Mayan Classical civilization can be described as happening between the years 200 CE and 1500 CE

5. COMPARE AND CONTRAST ELEMENTS OF INFORMATION

I. Purpose of a & b
II. How a = c
III. How a ≠ b

A depiction of the Puritan society as described in *The Scarlet Letter* and *The Crucible*.

6. LOCATE AND DESCRIBE TOPICS SPACIALLY

I. Locate and describe a
II. Locate and describe b
III. Locate and describe c

North Dakota can be described geographically as three regions: the Red River Valley, the Drift Prarie, and the Missouri Plateau.

7. INFORM OR PERSUADE BASED ON CATEGORIZED INFORMATION

I. Describe a
II. Describe b
III. Describe c [or persuade why a + b]

Prepare a rhetorical analysis of a famous speech such as "Letter from Birmingham Jail."

Audience

```
┌─────────────────────────────────────────────────────────────┐
│ DEMOSTHENOR TOOLKIT: AUDIENCE                     [□][─][×]  │
├─────────────────────────────────────────────────────────────┤
│                                                               │
│  ┌─────────────────────┐   ┌───────────────────────────────┐ │
│  │  Audience           │   │                               │ │
│  │                     │   │                               │ │
│  │  • How will you     │   │                               │ │
│  │    craft what you   │   │                               │ │
│  │    say in order to  │   │                               │ │
│  │    be understood    │   │                               │ │
│  │    (tone)?          │   │                               │ │
│  │  • How will the     │   │                               │ │
│  │    audience         │   │                               │ │
│  │    emotionally      │   │                               │ │
│  │    react to the     │   │                               │ │
│  │    message (mood)?  │   │                               │ │
│  └─────────────────────┘   │                               │ │
│  ┌─────────────────────┐   │                               │ │
│  │   Your Audience     │   │                               │ │
│  │                     │   │                               │ │
│  │                     │   │                               │ │
│  │                     │   │                               │ │
│  │                     │   │                               │ │
│  └─────────────────────┘   └───────────────────────────────┘ │
│                                               Jacob Carr, 2022│
└─────────────────────────────────────────────────────────────┘
```

"Who receives the message, and how will they react to it?"

1. Ask students to consider the real or imagined audience for a piece of writing based on tone and mood.

2. Next, ask students to practice writing in different styles for a given audience, trying to predict how they will receive it.

3. Finally, describe how to shift the tone, mood, and overall word choice used to fit the desired outcome better.

Example: Consider a student tasked with reading a speech on environmental conservation. When addressing elementary school students, the student adopts a warm and inviting tone, using simple language and vibrant imagery to create an inspiring mood. They might say, "Imagine our earth as a big, beautiful garden, where every plant and animal is happy and healthy because we take care of them!"

The same student then reads the speech to city council members. They shift to a serious and authoritative tone, employing precise terminology and citing compelling statistics to establish an urgent and persuasive mood. The revised opening might be something like this: "Esteemed council members, immediate action is required to mitigate the effects of climate change, as evidenced by the 15 percent increase in carbon emissions within our city, which demands our collective and decisive intervention."

Delivery

"What tools will you use to deliver the message?"

Practice this skill of understanding methods of delivery by giving students an imagined situation in which they will deliver content. Describe how you could use props, media, gestures, and volume to show the message better and achieve their goals.

Example: In a classroom setting, students are given the task of delivering a speech on the benefits of renewable energy. They are to utilize various delivery tools to enhance their message. One student decides to use a small wind turbine model as a prop to visually represent the concept of wind energy. They incorporate a slideshow of sunlit solar panels and flowing hydroelectric dams to reinforce their points. As they speak about the urgency of shifting away from fossil fuels, their gestures become more emphatic, and they raise their volume to convey the critical nature of the issue. When discussing the peaceful coexistence with nature provided by renewables, their voice softens, and their movements become gentle, mimicking a breeze. Through these tools, the student's delivery becomes a powerful conduit for their message, demonstrating the potential impact of well-executed speech delivery.

Environment

"In what setting will the material be delivered?"

How will a given setting affect how content is received? For example, what considerations must be made for delivering content in person in a large or small group, over digital means such as Zoom, and for varying lengths of time?

Example: For a speech on the importance of community gardens, students explore how different environments affect delivery. In a small group setting, the speaker sits among the listeners, fostering an intimate atmosphere where they can pass around seeds and soil, making the experience tactile and engaging. The proximity allows for quiet, contemplative discussion.

Conversely, for a large group in an auditorium, the speaker uses a microphone to ensure their voice carries. They might walk across the stage to engage different parts of the audience, making eye contact to create a connection despite the distance.

Speaker/Author

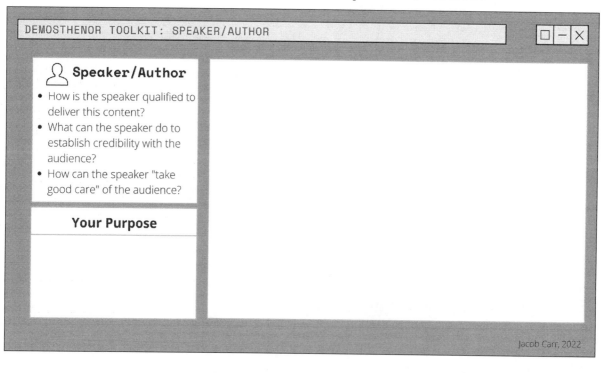

DEMOSTHENOR TOOLKIT: SPEAKER/AUTHOR

Speaker/Author
- How is the speaker qualified to deliver this content?
- What can the speaker do to establish credibility with the audience?
- How can the speaker "take good care" of the audience?

Your Purpose

Jacob Carr, 2022

"What is the speaker's purpose in delivering the material? To what ends are they working? How will they establish credibility with their audience?"

Practice describing the purpose and end outcomes of the speaking event. Determine how the author will create credibility:

- Why are they qualified?

Example: A local historian is invited to speak to a group of high school students about the importance of firsthand accounts in understanding history. They hold a PhD in history with a focus on oral histories, are a docent at a local museum, and have published several papers on the subject.

- Why is their goal?

    Example: The speaker's goal is for the audience to develop a love of local history.

- What is their commonality with the audience?

    Example: The historian relates to the audience by sharing historical stories of being a high school student in the area.

- Do they want the best for the audience?

    Example: Yes, the historian is passionate about local history and has found great worth in knowing about where they live. They want each individual to experience the satisfaction of sharing their own voice in the context of their history.

- Are they dynamic in their delivery?

    Example: The historian is known for their engaging, dramatic reenactments that help bring the historical events to life.

Key Points to Remember

Completing all parts of Demosthenor in one movement is a hefty lift! The true benefit comes not in the end product of a single speaking event but in the students' progress in specific skills over time.

Emily

Breaking it down like this is super helpful. If I had worked in smaller chunks like this for my public speaking class, I would have better understood my end goal and how to get there.

AP Adaptation and Correlation to Enduring Understandings

In the Demosthenor Toolkit EduProtocol, students enhance their oration skills, which are greatly valued in higher education and leadership, through a method akin to planning a significant event such as a wedding speech or marketing campaign. This protocol steers away from the usual clichéd presentation formats by employing scaffolding and templates to encourage practice. Repeated practice is recognized as a crucial pathway to achieving excellence. The toolkit addresses various components of speechmaking, including understanding the rhetorical situation, constructing claims with supporting evidence, employing reasoning and organization, mastering rhetorical style, and elucidating the functions of plot and structure. It also delves into the roles of narrators and speakers, the impact of word choice, imagery, and symbols, and the use of comparisons. Furthermore, students learn to develop textually substantiated arguments to interpret texts more deeply.

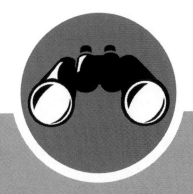

SECTION 3
Remixing and Revising

Chapter 14
Iron Chef Lesson EduProtocol Remixes

The Iron Chef Lesson EduProtocol is a four- to five-part jigsaw activity in which students create a digital slide artifact of their learning, combining "ingredients" given to them. (This EduProtocol is inspired by the popular cooking competition show *Iron Chef*.) The Iron Chef Lesson EduProtocol is an effective way to keep students on task and to cover content quickly. It is easy to implement, requires minimal preparation, and can be adapted to suit a wide range of subjects and grade levels.

In the classic Iron Chef Lesson EduProtocol, content is divided into four to five independent segments. For example, an educator utilizing the Iron Chef Lesson EduProtocol could break down the narrative elements into separate slides for a more focused analysis: one slide could examine how the setting influences the plot's development, another could delve into the symbolism woven throughout the story, a third could provide a detailed look at character portrayals, and a final slide could be dedicated to unraveling the story's central themes.

Each student is responsible for studying their designated segment and then creating a slide to explain that one piece. Each student also applies the idea of their secret ingredient, an unexpected or unique element that students must incorporate into each slide, further unifying the deck. Adding this ingredient is meant to challenge students' creativity and encourage them to think critically about how to integrate this component effectively into their work.

Jon

John Hattie's research says a jigsaw lesson has an effect size of 1.20. That's three years of growth. Jigsaw is #7 of Hattie's 256 researched pedagogies.

It could be a specific quote from outside of the resource, a primary source for further research, or a reflective image pertaining to the material that they need to use while they collaborate on creating their "dish," which in this case could be a presentation, project, or other educational artifact. Students then teach their slides to the whole class, creating a quick-paced and engaging learning experience.

In the original Iron Chef Lesson, students work in groups rather than individually. This allows them to collaborate and share their understanding of the material, which can lead to deeper and more meaningful learning.

Peer Review Remix

This remixed variation on the Iron Chef Lesson EduProtocol builds in peer review, which encourages students to recognize the connections between their own writing and that of their peers. This collaboration helps students identify their strengths and weaknesses and allows them space to grow without penalty. It also stimulates self-reflection and requires students to develop critical thinking.

Typically, educators find that peer review is ineffective because students get lost in the critique, "fix" things that weren't broken, or miss significant problems altogether. However, when peer review takes place in the context of lifting others up, instead of tearing them down, students work together to help the whole class's writing improve. Using the scaffold of an Iron Chef Lesson EduProtocol guides students systematically through the inquiry process and helps them to focus on ideas that you need to reinforce.

Academic Goals

Through successful implementation of the Iron Chef Lesson EduProtocol, students should be able to:

- Identify and evaluate claims and their supporting evidence
- Find alternate evidence
- Pose counterarguments

Teacher Big Ideas

By reviewing other students' work, students calibrate their expectations, see examples of how to complete a given assignment, and critically assess the structure and function of each other's work.

Prepare for the Activity

This EduProtocol should be implemented after students have completed a working draft of a piece of writing and are ready to make it even better. To prepare, create a peer review deck with the slides you want students to focus on. For example, you might direct students to complete a slide on a single facet of the assignment or rubric, or you might invite them to take a more in-depth look at multiple parts of the whole thing. If you're using a rubric for the final grading, select one or more of the criteria for peer review. Then, create a slide to house students' review of how their peers' drafts address each criterion. Some slides are prepared with a five-star rating so students can visually represent their opinion of the skills under assessment. You can, of course, choose to have your class use the five-star rating or not, as there are both rated and unrated slides available.

1. Ask students to prepare a draft of a piece of nonfiction writing for the EduProtocol.

2. Prepare an Iron Chef Lesson template deck with slides for the skills or goals you'd like students to assess.

3. Assign the template deck to students via your preferred method.

4. Students begin by pasting their writing sample to the resource deck.

5. They then share their deck with another student, who will review their writing and type answers to slide prompts into the deck.

6. When the slide deck is complete, the original author should have access to the deck so that they can make adjustments and corrections to their work. This is different from the classic Iron Chef Lesson, in which a group of students share a single completed deck; in this iteration, a single student benefits from the review of another student.

Instructions for Students

The Author

1. Copy your introduction to the resource slide. Make sure it's large enough to read easily.

2. Share this deck with a partner who will review your work.

3. When your partner's review is done, use their feedback to help edit your paper.

4. Turn your assignment in at Google Classroom.

The Reviewer

1. Add your name to the title slide under "reviewed by."

2. Begin by reading your partner's draft; just read it once to begin getting familiar with it.

Jake

Here's a template deck for your own peer review with the Iron Chef Lesson!

3. Next, for each slide, read the draft again, looking specifically at the questions posted.

4. When you're done, you will have read the resource multiple times. Don't just hunt for the answers to each slide prompt, skimming through; give your partner's draft a respectful read each time.

5. Whenever you offer feedback, give specific examples from the draft.

6. Be sure to complete the secret ingredient section, too.

Key Points to Remember

- Before implementing this EduProtocol, verify that students are already familiar with the material under review. The protocol is designed to strengthen existing knowledge and writing skills, not to introduce new concepts.

- Introduce the EduProtocol by reviewing small parts of drafts, such as an introduction. It is more beneficial to run this EduProtocol multiple times for a single piece of writing than to lump all the elements into one Iron Chef Lesson. As with all EduProtocols, onboarding is crucial. Repeat the process a few times as a class to clarify how it works, using a piece you prepared specifically for this purpose. (Poorly written fairy tales or Aesop's Fables [rewritten by the teacher] work excellently as first examples.) Working slowly at first will build capacities within the students for more extensive, complex work. By working together, you also build a culture of positive engagement, modeling how to review a piece of writing with a critical eye that does not cast negativity but instead inspires students to grow and build each other up.

Secret Ingredient Ideas

- A five-star rating on the slide

- An engaging or impactful quote from the source
- An emoji reaction
- A related but not covered topic

Variations

Instead of scouring the internet or Teachers Pay Teachers for just the right resource material, have AI write personalized articles for students to use according to the requirements and content of the Iron Chef Lesson!

Group Iron Chef Lesson

To scaffold this activity, give one example draft to each group. First, the group members review the sample based on assigned criteria. Then, they report back to the class. Next, a group introduces their review of a single criterion, and others add what they found. Each new group reports on another criterion.

Exquisite Corpse Model

This version happens in rounds. Begin by splitting up students into a number of groups equal to the number of criteria for the first round. Then give each group a different resource for the first round. Next, groups review their criterion, then pass their work and resource to the next group. The whole class works with a single criterion per round. This version can be done on paper or digitally in a shared slide deck.

- Group 1: The group reviews only the introduction.
- Group 2: The group reviews only the conclusion.
- Group 3: The group reviews the body.
- Group 4: The group reviews the overall grammar and mechanics.

By completing the Iron Chef Lesson peer review this way, each group becomes experts in their criterion by looking for the same elements across multiple resources. If you complete this several times with the same groupings, the whole class will eventually master the process for each criterion. This could be done with students' writings or with material you supply as the teacher. If you use a student's writing, consider using the work anonymously, or use work from a previous year's student.

Close Reading

Prepare for the Activity

1. Select a piece of writing for students to use.
2. Prepare an Iron Chef Lesson deck.
3. Provide a printed copy of the selection for students to annotate.
4. Assign as per your typical method.

Instructions for Students

1. Begin by reading the selection in the following ways:
   a) Quickly read through the material, almost skimming. Then, focus on the first and last lines of the paragraphs.
   b) Highlight the thesis of each paragraph in one color.
   c) Highlight the concluding statements of each paragraph in another color.
   d) Type the answer to the guiding question on the First Reading slide: "What is the main idea of this selection, and how do you know?"

Jake

Here's a template deck for your own peer review with the Iron Chef Lesson!

2. Begin your second reading of the selection by completing the following steps:

   a) Circle content-specific or unknown vocabulary (and write the definitions of these terms in the margin or as a comment).

   b) Underline evidence that supports the thesis.

   c) Note any patterns (chronology, ordinals, etc.).

   d) Type the answer to the guiding questions on the Second Reading slide: "How does the author craft this section? What keywords do they use? Is there clear evidence to support their claims?"

3. Begin a third reading of the selection by completing the following steps:

   a) Reread the text specifically for connections within the section. (Read paragraph to paragraph or within the section itself. Draw arrows connecting these elements.)

   b) Consider how the selection elements connect to ideas outside of the reading. (Draw arrows to the margin where you note allusions, references, and ideations.)

   c) Type the answer to the guiding questions on the Third Reading slide: "What is the author trying to convey? Do they do it well? What does the author want us to think after reading this selection?"

Secret Ingredient Ideas

- Take a picture of your annotations for each step and post it to the slide.
- Complete the phrase "I wonder . . ." and add an image.
- Incorporate a quotation from a secondary character that shows how they would view the material.
- Create a list of subject-specific vocabulary terms relevant to the topic.

Jon
The secret ingredient always thematically supports the content. It's never "share something funny."

- Add a multimedia component such as a video or sound clip that integrates meaningfully into the slide.
- Pose a thought-provoking question that doesn't have a straightforward answer.
- Connect the material to a current event that either parallels or contrasts the situation.
- Add a relevant quote from a classical philosopher.

AP Adaptation and Correlation to Enduring Understandings

Iron Chef Lesson has the potential to support all Enduring Understandings depending upon the prompts given.

By scaffolding writing through the year, the Mini-Report EduProtocol helps build writing skills and develop student capacity to write research reports.

In most classrooms, it takes students about four to six weeks to write a research paper, resulting in two to four reports per year. With limited exposure and without frequent feedback, lengthy projects can lead to engagement issues, procrastination, and stress, not to mention the heavy assessment load for teachers. This approach also falls short of preparing students for the quicker-paced research and writing in the professional world. While longer-form writing has its place, it needs to be interspersed with frequent shorter, targeted, skill-based activities that help build students' ability. For an in-depth discussion of this idea, see chapter 21 in this book, "Lifting EduProtocols."

The Mini-Report EduProtocol is structured to provide students with a quicker turnaround (more reps) on the essential skills they will need for longer reports. By engaging regularly in these activities, students build their research and writing capacities, making them more adept and ready to handle extensive long-form writing.

Jon

I got the idea from Rhonda Corippo as she explained the essence of report writing to our niece.

Marlena

I used a modified version of this Mini-Report EduProtocol with my sixth graders. It provided lots of reps and skill practice for my students and became a valuable piece of our writing practice and growth. It just makes sense as a scaffolded model.

The Thesis or Controlling Main Idea		

Chapters or Sections

Focus Area or *Supporting* Idea	Focus Area or *Supporting* Idea	Focus Area or *Supporting* Idea

Concept: Jon Corippo

Here is a simple organizer for students to collect their mini-report information. It's like an essay outline but more laid out in spatial ways.

Academic Goals

Through successful implementation of the Mini-Report EduProtocol, students should be able to:

- Combine facts from more than one source into one report
- Distinguish between relevant and irrelevant facts
- Build capacity for longer and more detailed reports over the course of the year

Teacher Big Ideas

- Model, model, model together on the board.
- This is a turn-and-burn writing assignment. If you take these home to grade, you're doing it incorrectly.
- Each Mini-Report is a quick write and is not to be revised or rewritten.
- Students should write in this format *every* week. After about six reps, students' skill increase will be noticeable. The first three or four reps may be slow to develop, but keep at it!

Prepare for the Activity

1. Choose two sources centered around one topic.
2. Prepare a fact-gathering sheet.

Instructions

1. Direct students to read the two sources and begin to collect facts and data on their fact-gathering sheet.
2. Solicit facts from the students and write them on the board.
3. Discuss the merits of the facts and their relevance to the report.
4. Ask students to add pertinent missing facts to their fact-gathering sheet.
5. Direct students to write three paragraphs based on the three focus areas.
6. After that, students should cite their two sources using an online citation machine.

Key Points to Remember

- The Mini-Report EduProtocol is a scaffolded approach to build student capacity throughout the year. As such, start

Feeling plucky? You can plug the students' pieces of evidence into a GPT model and have it return an outline for an essay or writing project. Give students time to analyze and revise.

small to build confidence before expanding into lengthier projects.

- Replace traditional essays and research projects for a quicker, more iterative process, thus allowing for more frequent cycles of feedback.

- This is designed for skill development. Therefore, assessment should focus on growth, not final product.

- Teacher involvement is critical in providing real-time feedback and modeling.

Variations

- Use a video for one of the sources.
- Include primary source documents as the basis for Mini-Reports.

Text Merge Remix

Students are tasked with integrating information from two different sources discussing the same topic into a single, concise plan for a one-page report. Initially, they should focus on three key thematic areas, which will be expanded to six by the year's conclusion, tailored to the grade level's requirements. The focus areas are thematic clusters where related information is grouped, such as a cluster called Presidents with subcategories like Childhood, Early Adult, Military History/Career, Presidency, and Legacy, or a cluster called Battles with elements like Location, Situation, Opposing Leaders, Outcome, and Legacy. These clusters help organize the facts into a structured narrative or argument.

Grading: At the early stage, focus on the task, not on the actual written product. The point of the Mini-Report in the first semester is to develop the skills needed to write the report, to find relevant facts, to interpret information, and to then merge information from two sources into one.

When grading Mini-Reports, look for the three most common errors, whatever they happen to be, and develop mini-lessons to eliminate those errors each week. Do not laboriously grade and mark up each paper; it saps your energy and does not produce student gains.

Consider these criteria for grading either a whole group or an individual:

- Is there a thesis?
- Are there five facts?
- Are the focus areas properly explored?

Adaptations for Developing Writers

- For some students, there is no such thing as a quick write; all writing is labor intensive. Remember that reps build fluency and skill level. Keep the source text content simple and short enough so all students can finish and feel good about their accomplishments.

- Read two resources about the same topic aloud (e.g., *I Am George Washington* by Brad Meltzer and *A Picture Book of George Washington* by David A. Adler). Together, choose relevant facts concerning one focus area and record them on the board, then have students write their Mini-Reports individually, based on the collective facts.

- If students are ready for more and their writing development can support another round with the same material, return to the same resources the following day. Reread and concentrate on a second focus area. Students will then add a second paragraph to their Mini-Report.

- For emergent writers, after a shared read-aloud and fact-finding session, each child should fold a paper into thirds and sketch a quick drawing (e.g., a stick figure) to illustrate three facts centered around one focus area. Encourage students to write a word or short sentence for each.

Marlena

This is different from beginning, middle, and end (BME) writing. In BME writing, students are focused on the sequence of events necessary for early comprehension. In the Mini-Report, students are focused on finding facts to support a key idea, which is essential to early writing.

- Use an age-appropriate informational video as the source material and watch it together.
- Developing writers can begin building the habit of citing sources by recording page numbers when they use books as a source.

AP Adaptation and Correlation to Enduring Understandings

In the context of AP English Language Arts courses, the Mini-Report EduProtocol directly supports several Enduring Understandings by providing students with frequent, focused practice in critical areas. It reinforces the comprehension of rhetorical context as students discern the purpose, audience, and constraints influencing the texts they examine. The protocol's iterative approach to synthesizing information from diverse sources sharpens evidence-based argumentation skills, essential for crafting persuasive analyses and coherent arguments. Students also engage deeply with the art of rhetorical analysis, evaluating the effectiveness of various rhetorical strategies employed within their sources. Furthermore, the Mini-Report facilitates the development of robust writing processes, as students draft, receive feedback, revise, and edit their work in a cyclical and reflective manner. This continuous practice fosters a deeper understanding of the complexity of authorial choices and the nuances of language, which are foundational to the AP English Language Arts curriculum.

Chapter 16
Random Emoji Power Paragraph EduProtocol Remixes

If you've ever tried out the Random Emoji Power Paragraph EduProtocol (REPP), you know what a fun and effective writing strategy it is. By presenting students with a random set of emojis, they identify the meaning of each one (don't belabor correctness here), then write a simple paragraph using one emoji per sentence.

At first, some teachers of older students shy away from this activity, considering it too simplistic or childish, but in my experience, students of every age enjoy it. I've used it with students in lower elementary grades but also with college students and adults. Sometimes it's great to get silly. And now it's even easier with the EduProtocols Random Emoji Generator on the EduProtocols website!

Jon

Get school-ready random emojis for FREE here: eduprotocols.com/class

Academic Goals

- Enhance creativity
- Practice writing cohesion between elements
- Develop inference skills
- Promote engagement

Teacher Big Ideas

- Use the novelty of emojis to engage students in writing.

Emily

An activity like this is an easy way to spark curiosity in a classroom. It's such a simple thing to do, and it can invite a lot of interest and make students feel more comfortable. As a senior, I can say that this is a fun activity for me, too!

- Promote risk-taking by encouraging students to find alternate meanings for emojis beyond their superficial symbol.
- Regular practice with this EduProtocol can increase students' writing fluency as they become quicker at generating ideas and constructing sentences within the structure.
- Recognize the value of joy in the process of education. This is meant to be fun.

Prepare for the Activity

1. Access the EduProtocols Random Emoji Generator or create a set of emojis to be used in this activity.
2. Set up a digital or physical platform for students to write and share their paragraphs. At the time of writing, Socrative is a favorite digital method. If you're going with analog, I like using 3-by-5 notecards that can easily be traded with other students.
3. Complete one round of Random Emoji Power Paragraph in front of the students, modeling how it works.

Instructions

1. Instruct students to write a paragraph using one emoji for each sentence in the order the emojis appear.
2. Encourage students to write creatively and stress that there are no wrong interpretations of the emojis.
3. One by one, generate or reveal the emojis either from the EduProtocols Random Emoji Generator or from your curated list.
4. Once paragraphs are complete, have students share their writing with the class or in small groups.

Key Points to Remember

- Emojis are just a tool for creative expression; there are no incorrect interpretations.
- Focus on the writing process and idea generation rather than grammatical perfection.
- Adapt the difficulty level by adding other criteria such as a list of vocabulary to be used, grammatical structure, etc.
- This is meant to build fluency and confidence in a fun, engaging way. If it becomes the means of assessment, it will lose some of its appeal and effectiveness as a learning tool.

Variations

Ridiculous Arguments

Try this remix out to infuse Random Emoji Power Paragraph with the power of argument! This way, students can practice crafting lightweight, silly arguments using a low cognitive load. After getting skilled at this, creating arguments that require a higher cognitive load can come more naturally to students. To turn the emojis into an argument, use the following scaffold:

- First emoji = thesis
- Second through fourth emojis = claims
- Fifth emoji = conclusion

For example, with a cowboy, mushroom, frustrated emoji, turtle, and golfer, a student could construct the following: "Embarking on life's journey with the adventurous spirit of a cowboy, we learn the importance of adaptability, even in dark times, facing our frustrations with resilience and embracing the steady, measured pace of progress. Just as in golf, where each stroke is a calculated step toward the final goal, our life's path, marked by these varied experiences, leads us to our personal achievements and successes, symbolized by the triumphant moment of reaching the final flag."

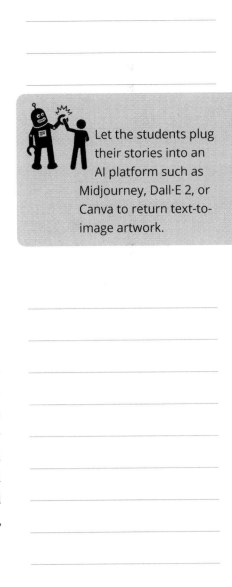

Let the students plug their stories into an AI platform such as Midjourney, Dall·E 2, or Canva to return text-to-image artwork.

Grammatical Scaffolds

Practice targeted constructions in grammar and style via this Edu-Protocol. Do this by overlaying restrictions to the Random Emoji Power Paragraphs. For example, tell students they can use only compound sentences, they must use at least one parallel construction, or they must use anaphora.

AP Adaptation and Correlation to Enduring Understandings

At first glance, the Random Emoji Power Paragraph might appear trivial, yet it has proved remarkably effective in fostering organic writing within a supportive framework that encourages self-expression, a skill sometimes challenging to cultivate in AP-level students. By incorporating structured elements such as sentence constructions and paragraph outlines, this activity allows students to practice formal writing in an informal setting. It can enhance their grasp of claims and evidence, reasoning and organization, and rhetorical style while also deepening their understanding of literary elements such as character, setting, plot, narrator, and the use of word choice, imagery, symbols, and comparison. Ultimately, it can guide students to construct well-supported arguments and engage in thoughtful interpretation of texts.

Created by Gamewright under the name Bring Your Own Book and adapted by Heather Marshall as Game of Quotes, this EduProtocol quickly became a favorite across many grades and content areas. It works great as an extension to silent reading, review, and so many other activities already happening in a classroom. The Game of Quotes EduProtocol addresses several challenges in the classroom. It reinvigorates silent reading and review sessions by transforming them into interactive, slightly competitive exercises that promote engagement and frankly, are fun. This EduProtocol solves the problem of students potentially becoming too focused on deep analysis to appreciate the text's language and surface features. By encouraging quick, frequent skims of a text, students learn to appreciate the craft of writing and recognize the nuances of language, character, and setting. Furthermore, it aids in the development of agile thinking, as students must swiftly connect prompts to textual evidence. This fast-paced approach can also enhance students' understanding of the text's structure, enabling them to navigate and extract information more efficiently, a vital skill in AP/College Board courses where understanding the construction of the text is crucial for deeper analysis.

In this EduProtocol's original form, students are given a short period to read or review a selection of readings. Next, the teacher presents a prompt such as "Songs from a terrible lullaby" or "Something that sounds creepy whispered." Students then skim the reading selection and choose a witty answer to the prompt.

Jon

GOQ makes SSR/DEAR time positively electric. I like to release all the possible questions before the read so the kids have them in mind as they read.

Once the first student has found a solution, a two-minute timer is set for the rest of the class. When the round is over, students share their answers. Many teachers report that letting the classroom vote for the best response increases the excitement of picking a winner.

Here are some fresh, new prompts:

- The punchline of a terrible joke told by a historical figure [note who it was]
- The inscription on a lost artifact, deciphered after centuries
- The final words of a dying alien sent to study humankind
- The cryptic warning label on a mysterious machine
- The most important rule of a forgotten secret society, passed down through generations
- The last line of a folk song, hinting at the deeper meaning
- The cryptic inscription on a ring passed down through generations, revealing a dark secret
- An insult that could start a war
- The inscription on a sundial showing not time but the number of lies told in its shadow
- Complete this title: "[Quote]: The Unexpected Wisdom of an Intergalactic Traveler"

Academic Goals

- Promote quick thinking and comprehension
- Practice critical thinking
- Build engagement with a text
- Foster creativity in academic work
- Engage in quick textual analysis

Teacher Big Ideas

- Encourage students to quickly think on their feet and make connections between prompts.

Emily

I remember this game from when I was in Carr's class. It was a huge hit with all of us, and it was really fun to try to win the title of "most creative quote" for the day.

Marlena

Game of Quotes is all about agile thinking!

- Foster a collaborative environment where students can share and discuss their chosen quotes, thereby understanding other students' insights.
- Recognize the intrinsic value of joy in learning.

Prepare for the Activity

1. Choose a text for use in the game. This could be a range of pages in a novel, the entirety of a short speech, etc.
2. Prepare prompts for the game. There are many available online and at Heather Marshall's website. You might consider forming these prompts into a slide deck or on 3-by-5 notecards.
3. Decide the means that students will use to share their quotes. This might be via an online platform or reading aloud.

Instructions

1. Instruct the students that a prompt will be read aloud. They will begin skimming the resource for an answer to that prompt.
2. When the first person who finds an answer raises their hand, start a two-minute timer.
3. When the timer is up, students share their answers. This might happen at table groups, and a table winner will be chosen. Then perform a second round to find the class winner.
4. Repeat with new prompts.

Key Points to Remember

- Game of Quotes is intended to be a quick-paced game.
- Focus the activity on specific parts of a resource in order to understand it better.

You can use AI to generate new and exciting prompts! You can also let students enter the quotes they chose and the prompts given, and AI will suggest other books they might enjoy based on their answers.

Variations

Reverse Engineering

As per a typical Game of Quotes, students are given a standard prompt. After finding their answer, students think of a new prompt for that evidence. Finally, students share their new prompt and evidence via Socrative, Padlet, a Collaborate Board on Nearpod, or a similar platform where students can vote for their favorite.

For example: Imagine the original prompt was "An unfortunate phrase to tattoo on oneself" and the winning response was "This has [. . .] been widely regarded as a bad move" (from Douglas Adams's *The Hitchhikers Guide to the Galaxy*). Next, students would be given the quote and have to come up with new prompts it could complement, such as "The secret message hidden in a children's bedtime story," "The fortune cookie message gone horribly wrong," or "The final words of a malfunctioning robot."

Serious Themes

1. Students are given a theme such as loss and transformation, humankind's relationship with nature, or coming of age instead of a standard prompt.
2. They are given time to search the internet and find evidence supporting the theme.
3. They then create a claim for the evidence.
4. Students share their new claim and evidence via Socrative, Padlet, a Collaboration Board on Nearpod, or a similar platform where the class can vote for their favorite.
5. The class votes for their favorite claim and evidence.
6. Once the top one to three choices have been decided, students should write an introduction paragraph that analyzes the claim and integrates the piece of evidence.

Example:

Students are given the coming-of-age theme. They are given time to search the internet and find evidence related to the theme. One student finds a quote from the character Elle Woods in *Legally Blonde*: "I graduated top of my class from UCLA. I believe young people can achieve anything they set their minds to." The student creates a claim that says: "The character Elle Woods's journey represents the struggle of coming of age." Students share their claims and evidence. The class votes and the *Legally Blonde* example wins. Students then write an introductory paragraph that analyzes the claim—how Elle Woods's journey to being taken seriously and overcoming stereotypes and self-doubt represents the struggle of coming of age. The introduction integrates the quote as evidence and sets up an essay exploring the theme of coming of age through personal growth in the face of adversity.

Marlena

Remember to onboard your students with content that is short, easy, and fun for all.

AP Adaptation and Correlation to Enduring Understandings

In an AP or college prep English class, texts are often studied formally and intensively. Students can become so focused on analyzing deeper meaning that they lose appreciation of the aesthetic beauty of the language itself. Playing Game of Quotes requires students to quickly skim texts multiple times, helping them map the surface-level construction of the work so they can later dive deeper into meaning and craft. This activity hits enduring AP understandings about claims and evidence, character, setting, word choice, imagery, and symbolism while aligning with UDL by offering multiple means of representation (quoting different textual passages), action and expression (constructing claims, sharing out), and engagement (gamification, peer interaction). By scaffolding literary analysis skills grounded in the text, Game of Quotes allows students to access challenging works while developing transferable skills for college readiness.

Chapter 18
Group Brainstorm EduProtocol Remixes

The Group Brainstorm EduProtocol helps students step away from their own thinking to see the thought patterns of another student. This activity is a great way to introduce a topic or begin a more formal writing project.

Working parallel with other students allows them to calibrate ideas and build off the ideas of another. It also helps weaker students scaffold their experience through the work of someone other than their teacher.

Academic Goals

- Promote critical thinking through interpreting an open-ended topic, making connections between ideas, and analyzing relationships within the ideas.
- Encourage collaboration through working together for a common goal, incorporating others' contributions, and building consensus.
- Enhance creativity of thought as students piggyback off each other's ideas.

Teacher Big Ideas

- The teacher should be a facilitator and not behave as a content expert.
- The open-ended format allows students to guide their own learning and explore their ideas.
- While a list of ideas is helpful in some instances, the real aim of this EduProtocol is the formation and development of brainstorming, making connections, and working together to build out ideas.

Prepare for the Activity

1. Develop an open-ended topic or prompt that engages students and connects across disciplines or real-world examples.

2. Decide a time limit for each phase.

3. Arrange the classroom to facilitate conversation.

Instructions

1. Prepare a slide with four columns for students to work in.

2. Copy this slide into a shared deck as often as you need for the number of students you have.

3. Direct students to choose a column to work in side by side with their peers and brainstorm as many entries as possible.

4. Encourage students to read the work of their peers and not copy but rather build off their ideas.

5. Encourage students to comment on others' works without verbal discussion.

6. After the allotted time, have students review the collaborative slide decks and reflect on patterns, trends, or surprises.

7. After students have reviewed the brainstorm, consider having them:

   ▸ Categorize and make connections between generated ideas.

   ▸ Use the ideas to make a creative product such as an infographic, poem, sculpture, etc.

   ▸ Develop a top-ten list of collaborative ideas.

You can use AI to brainstorm, too! Plug the prompt into a GPT model and paste the results into one of the columns alongside the student's work.

Variations

Writing Prompts

Present a writing prompt to students. Working in the four-column format, students use bullet points to present as many ways of answering the question as possible. Finally, they respond by writing a thesis statement.

Copia Thesis

1. Present a thesis statement on a prepared Group Brainstorm slide. Prompt students to rewrite the thesis statement in as many ways as possible without significantly altering the meaning of the original. Some possible shifts:

    ▶ Alternative word choice

    ▶ Changing pros/cons

    ▶ Reversing the order of clauses

    ▶ Adding or removing emphasis

    ▶ Using synonyms for key terms

    ▶ Changing the tone (e.g., from formal to informal)

    ▶ Altering the scope (broadening or narrowing the focus)

    ▶ Incorporating different perspectives

    ▶ Switching between passive and active voice

    ▶ Modifying the structure (e.g., compound to complex sentences)

    ▶ Introducing qualifiers or intensifiers

    ▶ Changing from abstract to concrete language

2. After rewriting the statement multiple ways, the class reflects on how altering the structure and word choice changes the tone, mood, and emphasis of the core argument.

    ▶ Example: Consider the following thesis: "Excessive smartphone usage negatively impacts teenage mental health, increasing anxiety, isolation, and distracted driving accidents." Students could rewrite it as such:

- Does excessive smartphone use undermine teenage well-being through heightened anxiety, loneliness, and unsafe driving habits? (Question)
- While smartphones provide some benefits, the overuse of this technology in adolescents correlates to more anxiety, less real-world interaction, and frequent car crashes. (Pro/con)
- Teenage mental welfare suffers from too much phone addiction, mainly through increased stress, lack of connection, and not paying attention while driving. (Alternative word choice)

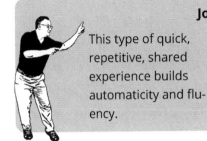

Jon

This type of quick, repetitive, shared experience builds automaticity and fluency.

Pieces of Evidence

Present a claim on a prepared Group Brainstorm slide. Then, task students with searching for evidence to support the claim. They might also present ideas for what kind of information would be found, such as "a source that shows x," to which another student could comment with keywords, a Boolean search operation, or a link to a resource they already found.

The Hive Mind

Each student creates a slide in a shared deck with their thesis statement at the top. Students work silently in the shared deck, interacting with other students' slides by posing questions for reflection as comments or offering pieces of evidence as bullet points on the slide. Students could use this work for a writing project.

AP Adaptation and Correlation to Enduring Understandings

In the often hypercompetitive nature of college preparatory and AP environments, collaboration can be seen as stealing ideas or even plagiarism. Using a Group Brainstorm activity not only helps students see alternate perspectives but also builds their schemas with the viewpoints of others. This collaborative behavior more accurately mimics real-world writing situations and helps foster teamwork.

Chapter 19
Internet Scavenger Hunt EduProtocol Remixes

Launched in the original book of EduProtocols, **Internet Scavenger Hunt helps students understand how to refine their searches and extract quality information from the seemingly endless content online.** With the exponential growth in web-based data and the use of AI, this process of searching and sifting has become even more critical. Students are often overloaded by search results and choose whatever is presented first. They often struggle to identify credible sources and narrow down their relevant information when exploring a topic.

The Internet Scavenger Hunt EduProtocol helps build strong research skills. By identifying and using keywords, using Boolean operators, and evaluating results, students build their critical thinking, healthy skepticism, and analysis capacities. The process also mirrors professional strategies data scientists and academics use to pare down massive data sets.

The world of search engines is changing! Try exploring platforms such as Consensus and other models that use AI to crawl peer reviewed journal databases.

Marlena

Start your year here! Make everything to follow a lot easier.

Academic Goals

- Evaluate key terms and search strategies critically.
- Encourage collaborative analysis of information.
- Facilitate finding strong evidence.

Teacher Big Ideas

- Search skills are vital to modern literacy.
- Focus on the process of inquiry, not just the product.
- Help students leverage the abundance of information available to them without being overwhelmed.

Instructions

1. Give students a topic to research via an internet search.
2. Direct students, either in teams or as partners, to search using key terms, aiming for as few results as possible while still yielding usable resources.
3. Finally, students should take a screenshot of their search results and present that image on a shared slide deck to be reviewed as a class.

Variations

Deep Mining Chains

- Limit students to sites such as Google Scholar or a similar academic search engine. Students should use key terms and search operators to find a few excellent articles on their topic as evidence. Each team member then chooses an article from that list to work with. Mining is done by using the bibliography of the article to lead to the next article and so on. This way, students dive deep into the research on a single strand of information.
- One way to use this method is to put students in groups and have each team member take a different claim of a single argument. By mining one argument together, students devise a chain of resources diving deep into the individual claims.

Jake

What is a Boolean operator? Boolean operators are search words such as and, or, and not, as well as punctuation such as quotation marks, parentheses, and asterisks that include or exclude search results, yielding more focused results. As AI gets better, Boolean operators will go away, but academic journals are slow to modernize in their searching. There's also a mental shift that happens when students think in these search terms.

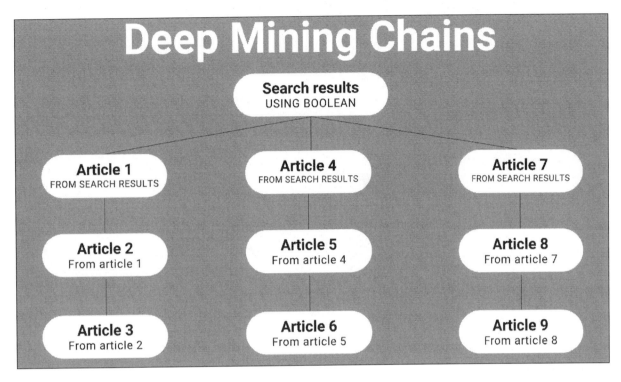

Limited Debate

Use the traditional version of Internet Scavenger Hunt, but make it even more purposeful.

1. First, present an arguable thesis to the class. Then, spend a few minutes discussing the topic so everyone has foundational working knowledge.

2. Next, divide the class into pro and con teams.

3. These teams will practice the skills of Boolean operator searches to come up with a list of search results (you will want to choose a maximum of results, perhaps ten to twenty).

4. Once students have their results, host an informal debate wherein they can use only those resources.

Source Citation

Once students have performed their Internet Scavenger Hunt, extend the learning objectives by having them create source cita-

Marlena

Kids are great at using their phones, but knowing how to conduct an intentional and careful search of information will unlock a whole new world!

tions for a number of the results. You might even have them create citations for a single resource in multiple formats (MLA, APA, Chicago, etc.).

AP Adaptation and Correlation to Enduring Understandings

Especially at a college preparatory and AP level, the ability to effectively and efficiently conduct research is critical. Often, we misdiagnose students as digital natives who don't need implicit instruction on how to use technology tools in more meaningful ways. By introducing strategies, we help students gain a skill that can benefit them for the rest of their educational journey and beyond.

SECTION 4

A Guide to Deeper Understanding

Chapter 20
Writing Projects: Rack and Stack

The ways AI can augment the writing process are nearly endless, from suggesting hooks, thesis statements, or relevant quotations to providing sample outlines, analyzing for feedback, and much more. The sky's the limit, so don't be afraid to let students interface with AI all along the way.

When you assign an essay to 150 humans and let them know it's due next week, several things are bound to happen:

- Students start calculating how long they can wait until they should begin working.
- You'll consider shifting the deadline if half the class needs more time.
- You'll be thinking about which, or how many, kids will plagiarize large swaths of their essays or just hand them over to AI.
- You'll probably block off some nights or weekends to spend grading all these essays once you've finally collected them.

These are problematic outcomes for many reasons. First, they undermine the learning and development of authentic skills. Calculating last-minute deadlines, plagiarizing, and taking shortcuts show that students are focused on simply completing a task rather than building the skills presented. Second, the workload created is taxing for teachers. A stack of 150 essays is overwhelming for proper assessment and ends up burning teachers out rather than helping them provide quality feedback. Finally, these dynamics create a strain on the teacher-student relationship rather than supporting learning through inspiration and purposeful scaffolding toward independence.

What if there was a better process for writing?

Educators can use Rack and Stack to pair and sequence Edu-Protocols into a process that fits their students' goals and needs, all while making writing instruction far more efficient for everyone, including the student and the essay grader (that's you). By using this scaffold, educators can create engaging and effective writing projects that will help their students develop their writing skills. No matter the writing task, stacking EduProtocols into a flow will yield great results.

We'll be using Rack and Stack on these EduProtocols:

Planning/Outlining

- Wicked Hydra (see chapter 4): This is an activity whereby students create branching questions like a mind map.

- Number Mania (see chapter 10 of *The EduProtocol Field Guide: Book 2*): In this activity, students create an info-graphic to demonstrate knowledge of a subject using numbers to tell the story of a historical event. They research for ten to fifteen minutes, submit numbers and facts through Google Forms, and the info is then transferred to Google Sheets and shared.

- Thick Slides (see page 105 of *The EduProtocol Field Guide: Book 1*): This is an extension of the Thin Slides EduPro-tocol where students present a deconstructed paragraph.

Content/Subject Matter Development

- Cyber Sandwich (see chapter 20 of *The EduProtocol Field Guide: Book 1*): Students work in pairs or threes, reading the same or different texts and noting their findings on Google Slides. After individual work, they collaborate to compare findings and create a summary slide of their ob-servations.

- Iron Chef Lesson (see chapter 26 of *The EduProtocol Field Guide: Book 1*): This is an EduProtocol version of a jigsaw.

Jake

There's a particular joy watching students real-ize that the work they've been doing magically converts into a nearly finished written proj-ect. By scaffolding the events, you can help students feel less leery of writing and find great pride in their finished product.

Jon

When you give feedback on a process students have executed many times in your class, grading the final ver-sion is a breeze because you've ensured quality all along the way. This is an approach I learned when I was teaching my film class. If I had waited until the end to see all the videos, we would have had weeks of cleanup.

- Number Mania (see chapter 10 of *The EduProtocol Field Guide: Book 2*): This is a streamlined activity where students create number-based infographics.

Editing and Proofreading

- Nacho Paragraph (a twist on the Random Emoji Paragraph from chapter 8 of *The EduProtocol Field Guide: Book 2*): The phrase "It's not your paragraph" plays on the idea that students edit a classmate's paragraph. It's a peer review exercise focusing on the editing process.

- For the People (this EduProtocol is unpublished at the time of this book's publication): This is a peer review process where students use a rubric or set of criteria to provide feedback on multiple peers' work, typically via Google Forms. Basically it is a gallery walk with Google Forms feedback from each student on overall poster accuracy, poster art, one thing the student really liked, and one thing they would change.

The New EduProtocols

The Process

1. **Planning and outlining:** Start with a **Wicked Hydra** from chapter 4 or **Number Mania** from chapter 10 of *The EduProtocol Field Guide: Book 2* to build excitement and background skills. This step involves setting goals, understanding the task, developing a thesis statement, organizing your arguments and ideas, creating an initial plan for the essay, and collecting resources. Another excellent option is having students do a series of **Thick Slides** where they can either be directed through the research or you can let them do free-form work. But here's the key: Students will build one Thick Slide in about

fifteen minutes per class period, meaning overall note-taking can be finished in about one-quarter of five class periods. Don't grade this, but give real-time feedback to individuals and the whole group on trends you see.

2. **Drafting:** Have students do a **Mini-Report** as their first draft/working copy. Another option is to have students do a series of singular paragraphs on a topic (**Random Emoji** style) with several rounds of **Nacho Paragraphs** to hone their work. The work students do in Socrative can be shared back to them via a spreadsheet that Socrative saves on each attempt.

3. **Sharing and revising:** Use a **For the People** EduProtocol to share and review students' feedback so that they can make changes to improve their essays' clarity, coherence, and overall effectiveness. You can teach students to make suggestions like rearranging paragraphs, cutting out unnecessary information, and clarifying arguments.

4. **Editing and proofreading:** Once students have revised their essays, they could use Grammarly or a similar checker to ensure they are grammatically correct.

5. **Finalizing and extending**: Students can publish or submit their essays. Then they can turn their essays into another product, such as a podcast, infographic, comic strip, or something else.

Depending on the complexity of your task, you might utilize one or many of the EduProtocols in each phase of the process. Next, I'll take you through three levels of complexity and how you can scaffold these writing projects.

Jon

Using a grammar-checking tool is a lifelong skill; I use one constantly. I also tell my students that I will be teaching them grammar and writing skills—but I'm not correcting their grammar on essays. They may not turn their essays in until they have fixed the grammar.

Fast Writing Task

For tests like those administered by the College Board, students will need to grasp a prompt, develop their thoughts, and self-edit between five and nine essays in a single sitting. They've likely not done this in any classes before yours., so it's important to help set them up for success by practicing these skills in a familiar environment.

Planning and Outlining

Planning on the fly is strongly enhanced by EduProtocols like the Random Emoji Power Paragraph. No one knows what's coming—not even you. For higher-level challenges, implement restrictions such as answers needing to be in second person, future tense, with at least one appositive sentence and a straw man argument, etc.

Drafting

Here's the beauty of an EduProtocols approach: Highly motivated students can easily execute three to four Random Emoji Power Paragraphs in thirty minutes or less. Give real-time feedback on the target objectives of the activity and then prompt students to do another rep immediately. Fast feedback equals fast growth. And since you're giving feedback in real time, there's nothing to grade after school. Additionally, since you're engaging your students, the AI/copy-paste monster is kept from class.

Sharing and Revising

Sharing and revising will happen three to four times daily over the course of the assignment. You can end each Random Emoji cycle with a Nacho Paragraph to easily gauge the class's skill at revision and iteration in real time.

Editing and Proofreading

Encourage students to review drafts for grammar, coherence, and prompt adherence. Provide a checklist or guidelines for this process. Students can use AI tools for feedback, enhancing their writing quality and clarity. Emphasize self-editing and peer feedback to refine their essays. The purpose is to have another rep and another iteration of the process that gives students a chance to get better each time, not to strive for perfection.

Finalizing and Extending

The goal here is to help students write with greater agility and adaptability. After three to five days of reps, students can select one of their favorite drafts from the week and develop a deeper and longer two- to three-paragraph essay in class. The time-restricted nature of this exercise is key. Students get twenty to thirty minutes to write, modeling what they'll need to produce for college admissions tests.

A Moderate Writing Task

Perhaps you want to spend more time crafting a written project to further develop the skills students have been working on. Using larger-form projects from time to time helps with this. For a deeper conversation about this, read the "Lifting EduProtocols" chapter at the end of this book. But for now, let's look at some scaffolding for this process.

Planning and Outlining

As a class, conduct:

- **Wicked Hydra** on the topic. This will help students select questions to use as a foundation for their writing. Students choose one of the questions and turn it into their thesis.
- **A Frayer Model** to review the writing task and rubric and set parameters for students' writing, such as who the audience will be, the complexity of style, etc.
- **Walk the Line** to analyze an argument.
- **Iron Chef Lesson** to segment topics.
- **WHASH** to look specifically at the rhetorical situation or **Cyber Sandwich** to compare two resources. Each of these creates a paragraph that can be incorporated into a final written piece.

Drafting

Students take the material created in the planning and outlining phase and combine it into the body of their written work.

Combine **Walk the Line**, **Claim Jumper**, and **WHASH** to scaffold students' thinking. Students then write their introductions and conclusions as bookends to the prewritten body material.

Sharing and Revising

For this phase, students look at each other's work, either in whole or in part. I like to focus on introductions. You could have students write or print out just the introduction in the middle of a piece of paper and perform a **Wicked Hydra**. This will help students understand the perceived scope of their writing so they can align it with the assignment prompt.

An **Iron Chef Lesson** peer review lets students share their work with other students to gain feedback and revise accordingly.

Editing and Proofreading

In this portion of the stack, students take feedback from their peers and instructor and evaluate it. Not all feedback is good feedback. Deciding what they will change is intrinsic to students' development as writers. I also find that working with pen and paper is beneficial for the final proofreading task, and it's also an excellent way to see how in depth students' edits are.

Finalizing and Extending

As an extension, students may adapt their finished writing project into an infographic, comic, or fishbowl defense activity. **Demosthenes Toolkit** is also an excellent place to drop parts of the material to extend students' ideas into an oral presentation, even if students don't deliver the oral address.

An In-Depth Writing Task

Sometimes, as outlined in chapter 21, "Lifting EduProtocols," it's time for a heavy lift, where you want students to dive into a writing process. EduProtocols stack well for this type of assignment, and they guide students to deeper understandings of the topics they explore in their writing. For the example assignment that follows, this heavy lift unfolds through a sequenced process. First, students will explore the topic using Thick Slides, progressing to collaborative inquiry with **Shared Research** and the **Wicked Hydra** DOK model. After building this foundation, students move into a multifaceted essay by using **Walk the Line** and **Claim Jumper** to arrange their arguments. This is followed up with **Iron Chef Lesson**, **Nacho Paragraph**, and **YPMG!** as peer reviews and a reflection. Each step is designed to build on the last, scaffolding student learning and writing and pulling in all the previously developed skills in a way that is both structured and explorative.

Planning and Outlining

Begin by introducing the topic of the argument. Students can watch a short video about the topic and complete a Thick Slide (four to five bullet points of information, an image, a quote, and a summary thesis of what it's all about).

Next, using a platform such as Socrative, have students develop and pose a follow-up question about the topic. Hold a vote to discern the five most interesting questions. These become the five central themes used for the remainder of the project. Students will engage with these themes using the **Wicked Hydra** DOK model, where they deepen their inquiry by asking more detailed and complex questions. As a final step, each student will select the most intriguing high-level question from one of the themes to write about further.

Next, students should complete a **Shared Research EduProtocol** on all the themes previously explored. In this EduProtocol, students curate resources from the internet and compile them into a shared spreadsheet by inputting the information into Google

Forms (citation of resource, description/summary, domain in a drop-down menu). This becomes a curated list of resources for them to use for the remainder of the project.

Students need to review the writing prompt and rubric that you supply. I like doing this after the initial research starts, but you might do otherwise. Students should complete a Frayer Model outlining their goals for the writing process, such as how many different sources they will utilize, the intended complexity of the writing, the audience they are writing for, etc. This is also the time for students to craft their thesis statement based on the question they chose from **Wicked Hydra**, as it will drive their work from here forward.

Once students know where they're headed, it's time to let them use their tools. Students can begin by creating an outline of their finished essay as a standard form argument. They should use **Walk the Line EduProtocol** to craft their argument, which will help them plan their claims and rhetorical choices.

After that, students should dive into their shared research data to identify sources they can use to support their argument. They can use **Claim Jumper** to evaluate each resource, then integrate specific pieces of evidence into their **Walk the Line** deck.

Drafting

Once students have a solid outline of a sound argument with backing, they should begin writing. Running a **Walk the Line EduProtocol** facilitates this well, as they can take each claim slide and write it into a body paragraph. After stacking these together, they should write a cogent introduction and conclusion for a finished draft.

Sharing and Revising

When students have a working draft, they should complete a peer review version of the **Iron Chef Lesson**. This is where I also like to enter specific points of feedback. Along with peer review and completing a self-reflection on goals, a **Frayer Model** is a great tactic to keep students in alignment with their aims. Using these two

EduProtocols, students should make any major revisions to their writing, such as addressing paragraph order, getting rid of a source that doesn't work and replacing it with something better, etc.

If you want to dive deeper, students can perform protocols like **Nacho Paragraph**, where they peer edit each other's introductions or conclusions. Even just sharing their outlines with multiple peers can be beneficial, helping students to double-check their line of reasoning.

Editing and Proofreading

Students should take all the feedback they've been given, evaluate it, and make changes to their drafts.

Finalizing and Extending

After finalizing their written work, students complete a **YPMG! EduProtocol** to evaluate their successes and struggles. This is also the time to extend students' process to publishing their ideas via an infographic, speech, short-form video, or another form of work. Transforming their written piece into another format helps students see the benefits of thoughtfully planning and researching something before sending it out into the world.

Key Points to Remember

- Keep students moving quickly.
- It's more effective to see progress over multiple repetitions than to belabor one perfect round.
- Personalize microteaching lessons for the development of individual skills that need practice. These foundational skills will support the more complex tasks in larger projects. You don't have to take writing projects to completion every time. I've found great benefits in cycling through the planning phase, where the finished product is a detailed outline. Once students have made several of these, they can choose one and further develop it.

Make your own Rack and Stack processes. Below is a menu to help you plan out your projects:

Stage	Focus	EduProtocols
Planning and Outlining	· Consider goals · Know the audience · Understand the task · Review the rubric or evaluation tool · Conduct research · Prewrite · Craft the thesis · Create an outline	· Frayer Model · Claim Jumper · Shared Research · WHASH · Group Brainstorm · Iron Chef Lesson · Wicked Hydra · Cyber Sandwich · Walk the Line · Nacho Thesis · AnnoTwist · Thick Slides
Drafting	· Build out the thesis · Write body paragraphs · Write the introduction and conclusion	· Random Emoji Power Paragraph · Mini-Report · Previously written work from the planning and outlining phase
Sharing and Revising	· Read through yourself · Conduct peer review · Gain feedback from peers and instructor · Evaluate your work after sharing	· Iron Chef Lesson (peer review) · For the People · Wicked Hydra (for introductions) · Nacho Paragraph (for segments of the written work) · YPMG!
Editing and Proofreading	· Evaluate feedback · Apply feedback as desired · Make edits	· For the People · Nacho Paragraph
Finalizing and Extending	· Reread · Extend · Infographic · Short-form video · Fishbowl · Oral presentation · Comic strip · Podcast · Etc.	· Demosthenor Toolkit

There are critical moments in life when you realize you are completely and utterly out of your depth and at the mercy of a foreign environment. That was my experience a few years ago. After months of physical therapy following shoulder surgery, I found myself recommended to a little gym at the back of an industrial complex. The first acolyte I saw was an ox of a human with a low-shaved mohawk and muscles as impressive as his thick black beard, who was jumping out of a Chevrolet Suburban with flames painted on the sides. Honestly, flames. I closed the door to my economical and sensible commuter vehicle, enshrouded myself in the armor of a lifetime of feeling weak and overweight, and entered a type of temple at which I had never been a practitioner.

At once, I experienced the aura of sweat, chalk dust, and smelling salts. The grunts and groans of temple-goers, chimes of steel and iron, and often blush-inducing sermons were carried on a wind of gangster rap, German heavy metal, and '80s technopop like prayer incense out the roll-up bay doors at the back and to the orchards beyond. I felt like Dorothy, and this sure as heck wasn't Kansas anymore. And then I met the wizard.

Coach Michael Headley, never Mike, absolutely not Mikey, is a bulldog of a man. An "Alabama Cuban boy," he calls himself. Bald. Bearded. Looks like a vial of testosterone. He's not tall; he doesn't need height to tower over people. He's witty and wicked intelligent. But, more importantly, he knows what he's doing thanks to decades of experience and study. Imposing at first glance, he smiles, and you're somehow not afraid of what you don't know.

"You must be Jake-ee." He grinned with a warming chuckle, knowing my sister had slipped a torturous childhood nickname into his arsenal. "Let's get you on the sled."

Jon

This was my exact experience playing D1 football at Fresno State as a 160-lb. lineman. The judgment is real!

Contemplating the metal sled he meant for me to drag around a parking lot, I felt weak and lost; if I had been handed a rubber chicken and asked to stand in a corner, I might have considered it. But instead, this man was the gateway to redemption from weakness and pain. This man was my redemption from feeling physically broken. As I would soon find out, this man was the high priest of his temple, with decades of experience and training to back his muscles and puppy-like grin. Coach was going to help me save myself. But I had stepped into calculus and been handed a primary number line.

Since beginning that cold day in February, I've continued lifting four days a week. My little group, the Six O'clock Crew, meets before sunrise to grow and develop our physical and mental capacities. We're not alone in the gym. Along with Coach, the former minotaurs and shield maidens of my introduction have dropped their avatars to become professionals with bad Yoda impersonations, law officers, teachers, and even elite-level athletes who hang their medals by the front door in a heap.

But why am I asking you to read all about the sport of powerlifting in a pedagogy book? Because they share the same principles.

As educators, we ask students to enter temples of development where they feel foreign, incapable, and even shunned due to previous experiences. They can feel weak in the presence of others, and sometimes we make them feel broken. The first time I did a hammer curl, I was hyperaware that my tiny dumbbell paled compared to the mass hefted next to me. But my shoulder dictated that three pounds were what I needed. After following Coach's teachings and plans, I've developed balanced strengths I didn't know I had. And that intimidating mohawked man from before? One day, he noticed what I was lifting had increased, kindly helped correct my form, and commented, "Weren't you using three-pounders just a little bit ago? Nicely done, man." Because, in the gym, it's about growth. We're all chasing the next step. As Coach puts it, we aren't there to exercise; we're there to train because "exercise is activity based, but training is end-outcome based."

How often are our classrooms activity based? We flit like bees from one activity to the next, one worksheet to another, hoping that the accumulated time spent on tasks amounts to something passable on a state test. Or we follow the prescription of a pacing guide handed to us by the council of publishers. But are we exercising or training? I have two ideas I would like to explore: *compound versus isolated movements* and the practice of *periodization*.

Compound versus Isolated Movements

In resistance training, the two primary forms of movement are *compound* and *isolated*. Compound movements, such as the squat, deadlift, and bench press, mobilize multiple large groups of muscles and joints to move an object through space. Isolated movements, such as hammer curls, crunches, and lunges, focus their mobilization on single joints and muscle groups in a targeted expression. For example, the deadlift (compound) uses the trape-

Jon

Want to get geeky on Jake's claim? Look up the Ebbinghaus effect. It's a real thing. We don't esteem this behavior in education, yet we bemoan when students don't "know" things they should.

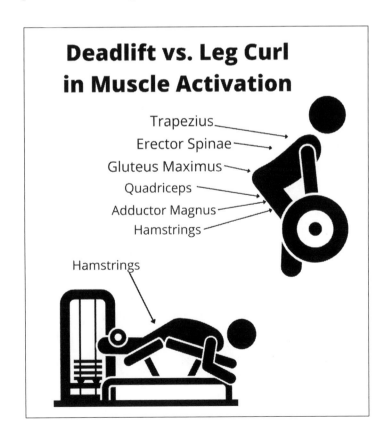

Jon

Fancy education term: recursion. This is memorizing patterns, like driving a stick shift car (that's a nonautomatic car for the millennials).

zius, erector spinae, gluteus maximus, quadriceps, adductor magnus, and hamstring muscles, which make up the entire posterior chain. In contrast, a lying leg curl (isolated) uses, for the most part, only the hamstrings.

The true art of training is knowing that you don't need to only practice deadlifts. Coaches know that a deadlift comprises a significant leg movement followed by a hip movement. Those two movements can be isolated into a leg press and kettlebell swing.

By working on individual actions, the mobilization and ability to do work in the deadlift increase.

This distinction is not unlike skills development in our classrooms. After years of teaching, I know that you don't get better at writing essays by writing more essays but by crafting outlines, working on transitions, constructing paragraphs, honing grammar, examining tone and mood, etc. These isolated classroom movements add to the practice of crafting better essays without belaboring it. Please understand me: Compound movements such as rhetorical essays, literary analysis, or public speaking events are fundamental and, in the end, represent the application of our craft. Still, we can focus efficiently on isolated movements to hone the skills required for these practices.

By taking the classic compound lifts of English Language Arts and purposefully breaking them down into their components, we can more efficiently develop skills. I polled my sophomore English classes about their growth over the semester. Overwhelmingly, sections reported the same: they had become much better at writing essays. I found this anecdotal data funny at first, and it wasn't until the next day that I asked them how many essays they thought they had written that semester. Each class thought back, guessing six, eight, ten. They were shocked to learn they had only been assigned one essay that semester. We wrote a lot. We wrote often. We wrote dozens of introductions, outlined countless ideas and paragraphs, argued conclusions, and performed so many other movements. But we practiced isolated skills building up to the whole essay in December. And those essays were good, which brings up my second point.

Periodization

Considered the greatest coach in Soviet history, Alexander Sergeyevich Prilepin led the weightlifting world and revolutionized how athletes train. Through decades of research involving over a thousand elite-level Russian athletes, Prilepin honed a system of training still touted as the most effective way to build strength: the Prilepin chart of periodization. In resistance training, periodization is the manipulation of training variables such as weight, number of repetitions, number of sets, etc., to prevent overtraining and develop more extraordinary skill sets and capabilities. By training for several weeks at between 70 percent and 90 percent of what they were capable of, athletes being trained by Prilepin maximized their gains, leading them toward a staggering twenty-seven world records between 1975 and 1985. He also found that first working well below 70 percent of their maximums for the first rep was the ideal way for athletes to build endurance and muscle memory. This trained the athlete to complete the movement with good form.

From this idea, periods were formed where athletes train for several weeks at a lower weight level but do the activity more times. After a period, they shift toward higher weight with fewer reps, moving through Prilepin's recommendations of 70 percent to 90 percent. By moving the balance of weight and repetitions, athletes see more significant gains in endurance and strength than they would have had they just lifted heavy weights the whole time. At the end of their cycle, they retest what they can, discovering their new one-rep maximum. From there, they begin the process again at the appropriate percentage of their new capacity.

How often do we present students with a heavy lift at the beginning of their training? Or even worse, we expect them to perform beyond their capacity, elevating the risk of injury? In the classroom setting, "injury" comes from straining toward skills and activities that are too challenging for a student's present level. This can lead to mental fatigue, loss of motivation, lack of confidence, and an overall malaise in education much like physical strain in a gym can lead to bodily injury and derailed progress. We don't want

Marlena

Exactly! Cycling through challenging tasks with slightly easier tasks interspersed allows students to have a moment to grow without the frustration that results from a succession of complex tasks.

Jon

My football coach said this a hundred times to us: Reactions are what you do without thinking. You get the correct reactions by doing a million reps.

students to associate education with stress and anxiety rather than growth and discovery. This will diminish their love of learning.

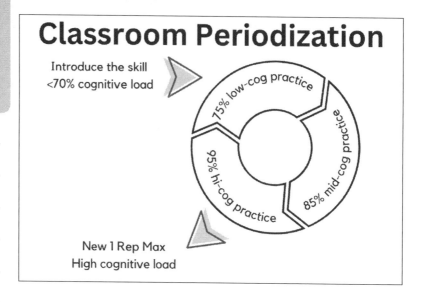

Classroom Periodization

Introduce the skill
<70% cognitive load

75% low-cog practice

85% mid-cog practice

95% hi-cog practice

New 1 Rep Max
High cognitive load

We could see a benefit by implementing some of the principles of Prilepin's chart in our classrooms. When we introduce a new skill, workflow, EduProtocol, etc., we should do it in a simple, fun, playful way. Doing this with a low cognitive load allows a student to practice the movement without struggling against the content. This is a tenet mindset of the EduProtocols. Every time we show the students a new EduProtocol, we do it in a silly and straightforward way. We do parts and pieces of it if need be. We do this to train them to accomplish the task, build a healthy relationship with the activity, and grow endurance. Then, once they have a level of comfort, we jump into the content and aim for the denser zone of proximal development. By using intermediary and purposeful steps between onboarding and struggling, we help students grow. We train students using more reps with lower cognitive loads, like training at 75 percent of the most challenging task they can complete, then shifting through 85 percent and 95 percent as more complex tasks are done less often. If we cycle through this a few times before asking the students to really "grunt and strain," their overall growth can be more significant, and we get a more accurate assessment of their current ability. And in my experience, spending time on the lighter side of the ZPD increases stamina. The student is more likely to foster a positive relationship with the content before pressing against what they are capable of. This dance between "I think I can" and "easy-peasy" pays off in the end.

Periodization with Compound Lifts and Accessories

But how do we put these principles of weightlifting together in the classroom? In a training session, athletes begin by doing a compound lift at a programmed percentage, followed by isolated accessories designed to strengthen the compound lift. Here is an example from my workout this morning. We began by bench pressing 80 percent of our maximum six times and repeated this set five times, resting in between. It was genuinely hard. After the bench press (compound), which utilizes most of the major muscle groups of the upper body, we isolated muscle groups. This was done individually with Tate presses, seal rows, lat pulldowns, and chest fly exercises. We'll continue moving through Prilepin's chart until we retest our bench press maximum at the end of our sixteen-week progression to see our development.

We can apply this system in many purposeful ways in a classroom. For example, we may want the students to increase their ability to write a rhetorical analysis of a political speech. Such a task is compound in nature, comprising parts such as the ability to recognize claims and evidence, an understanding of rhetorical choices, word choice analysis, discernment of the validity and soundness of the line of reasoning, standard grammatical and mechanical constructions, and so many others. Instead of jumping in with a prompt to simply analyze the speech, which requires a particular insight, endurance, and skill ability, we look at something more approachable. For example, we might start with a *Calvin and Hobbes* cartoon, using it to practice a few of the skills listed above. After doing this a few times, we up the cognitive load by moving to a more complex political cartoon, then group work, and so on, in-

AI-powered platforms can analyze individual students' strengths, weaknesses, and learning preferences to create personalized learning pathways. These pathways can include targeted exercises (isolated movements) focusing on specific skill development before progressing to more complex tasks (compound movements). By tailoring instruction to each student's needs, AI can support the periodization approach described in the text.

Jake

After writing this, I kept up with my workout progression and added five pounds to my bench press, fifteen pounds to my squat, and fifteen to my deadlift. Periodization works!

Marlena

Reps lower cognitive load. With reps, speed increases. Creativity increases. Swagger makes an appearance.

Marlena

Moving from a comic such as *Calvin and Hobbes* to a complex political cartoon to a political speech is a perfect EduProtocols skill flow!

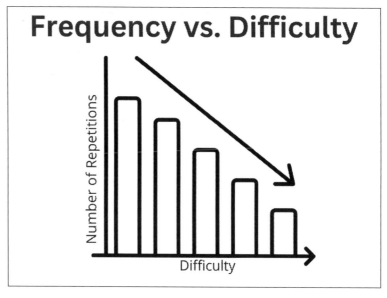

It's important to remember to scale how often something is done with how difficult it is in order to reap the benefits of growth without exhaustion.

creasing the difficulty but decreasing the number of activities until the students' capacities are built. Finally, we ask them to "grunt and strain" against the compound activity.

#PrilepinsClassroom

This is not a period but rather the first clause in a complex thesis in development. What do you think? What do you know? I would love to consider this an open call for dialogue. Let's take over the hashtag **#PrilepinsClassroom** and think about this on social media platforms. Is it reasonable? Is it valid? What does the research have to say?

See you at the gym.

Want to Learn More about Using EduProtocols in Your Classroom?

Ever wished you could pick the brains of the EduProtocols pioneers? Now you can at EduProtocolsPlus.com!

One price for a lifetime of support!

- **Reusable templates** with regular additions
- **Exclusive live and recorded shows** featuring EduProtocols authors and experts
- **Self-paced courses**
- **Supportive community**
- **Discounts** on online, face-to-face PD, and Summer Academies
- **District plans** available

EduProtocolsPLUS.com

EduProtocols books for teaching and leadeship

Appendix
UDL Breakdown

Engagement

1. **Game-Based Learning**: Use EduProtocols like the Random Emoji Power Paragraph and Fast and Curious to increase student engagement and motivation, especially for those struggling with traditional learning.

2. **Feedback Mechanisms**: Encourage peer feedback through EduProtocols such as Iron Chef Lesson, promoting metacognition and self-regulation to help students evaluate their understanding and identify areas for improvement.

3. **Collaborative Flexibility**: Allow students to work individually, in pairs, or in small groups, providing flexibility in engagement with content.

Multiple Means of Action and Expression

1. **Rhetorical Summaries**: Have students write detailed rhetorical summaries or précis, as in the AnnoTwist and We Have a Situation Here EduProtocols, to express their understanding in their own words, identifying and analyzing the author's rhetorical choices and techniques.

2. **Varied Prompts**: Offer different prompts and ways for students to show their final analysis, such as through writing, digital presentations, or discussions, as seen in the 3x Challenge EduProtocol.

3. **Creative Learning**: Use activities like assigning emojis to represent characters' strengths and weaknesses through the Unto the Breach EduProtocol to encourage playful and creative exploration of content.

4. **Vocabulary Strategies**: Employ strategies like the Frayer Model, allowing different expressions and vocabulary development, supported by EduProtocols like Repuzzler and Fast and Curious.

Multiple Means of Engagement

1. **Scaffolded Activities**: Provide scaffolded, easy-to-reproduce formats for tasks like close reading and annotation, making them engaging and relevant to real-world scenarios, as demonstrated in the Cyber Sandwich and Iron Chef Lesson EduProtocols.

2. **Gamified Processes**: Incorporate gamification, physical movement, and collaborative work to maintain student engagement and motivation, as seen in The Fast and the Curious, Wicked Hydra, and Repuzzler.

3. **Diverse Interaction Opportunities**: Use group work, gallery walks, and online quizzes to facilitate peer learning and keep students engaged, which can be integrated through EduProtocols like the Internet Scavenger Hunt, Fast and Curious, and Game of Quotes.

Multiple Means of Representation

1. **Visual and Spatial Organization**: Use template decks for visual organization of material, allowing students to present their analysis in various formats, such as writing or video responses, exemplified in the Thick Slides and Mini-Report EduProtocols.

2. **Multimodal Resources**: Include a variety of resources (texts, videos, audio, comics, artwork) to cater to different learning styles, supported by all EduProtocols.

3. **Nonlinguistic Representation**: Encourage students to use iconography and images to represent vocabulary and concepts non-linguistically, aiding in understanding and retention, as seen in the Ikonic, Repuzzler, Thin Slides, and so many more EduProtocols.

Options for Self-Reflection and Self-Regulation

1. **Reflective Activities**: Allow students to reflect on their learning process, set goals, and adjust their approach based on feedback through EduProtocols like YPMG! and Demosthenor Toolkit.

2. **Flexible Pacing**: Let students work at their own pace and choose which words or concepts to focus on, promoting self-regulation and management.

Appendix
Transferable Skills

The study "Defining the Skills Citizens Will Need in the Future World of Work," published in June 2021, was conducted by McKinsey & Company to address the rapidly evolving landscape of work due to digital and AI technologies. The COVID-19 pandemic further accelerated these changes, making it crucial to understand the specific skills that will be essential for future workers. The study surveyed eighteen thousand people across fifteen countries to identify fifty-six foundational skills, termed DEL-TAs (Distinct Elements of Talent), that will be necessary for citizens to thrive in a more automated, digital, and dynamic labor market. Keeping these transferable skills in mind when planning our classes is essential to ensure students are well-prepared for their future.

In this appendix, we align sample EduProtocol activities with essential transferable skills, as identified by the McKinsey Global Institute. These fifty-six foundational skills encompass cognitive, digital, interpersonal, and self-leadership categories. This list is not exhaustive but serves as a starting point for infusing our classrooms with these critical skills. By integrating EduProtocols with these skills, we provide a comprehensive approach to teaching that not only engages students but also equips them with critical abilities such as adaptability, critical thinking, collaboration, and digital fluency. There are many more examples of how skills are practiced through EduProtocols, and while not all of the fifty-six are listed here, they could certainly be aligned. This alignment ensures that our educational practices are preparing students to add value beyond automated systems, operate effectively in digital environments, and continually adapt to new ways of working, thus future-proofing their careers.

The research aimed to provide a precise definition of these skills to aid governments in developing curricula and learning strategies. The study found that higher proficiency in these DELTAs is linked to better employment prospects, higher incomes, and greater job satisfaction. This insight is intended to help shape education and adult training systems to better prepare citizens for the future of work. While this is only one resource for understanding and implementing soft skills, it is, in my opinion, a good one. I encourage you to find the study and familiarize yourself with it, as it contains much more detailed and usable information.

Transferable Skill	EduProtocols That Practice This Skill
Adaptability	Fast and Curious Random Emoji Power Paragraph Wicked Hydra
Active Listening	8 p*ARTS Demosthenor Toolkit Thin Slides
Agile Thinking	Random Emoji Power Paragraph Wicked Hydra
Asking the Right Questions	Wicked Hydra
Collaboration	Repuzzler Iron Chef Lesson CyberSandwich
Creativity and Imagination	Thin Slides Random Emoji Power Paragraph Game of Quotes Sketch and Tell
Critical Thinking	Repuzzler Iron Chef Lesson Walk the Line We Have a Situation Here
Data Literacy	Number Mania
Digital Collaboration	Iron Chef Lesson Cyber Sandwich Thin Slide Study Guide
Logical Reasoning	We Have a Situation Here Game of Quotes Parafly Claim Jumper

Transferable Skill	EduProtocols That Practice This Skill
Seeking Relevant Information	Mini Report Internet Scavenger Hunt
Self-Confidence	Demosthenor Toolkit
Storytelling and Public Speaking	Thin Slides Mini Report Demosthenor Toolkit
Structured Problem Solving	3x Challenge Number Mania
Synthesizing Messages	Parafly Frayer Model Mini Report Cyber Sandwich
Translating Knowledge into Different Contexts	3x Challenge Game of Quotes Worst Preso Ever
Work-Plan Development	Iron Chef We Have a Situation Here Claim Jumper

Acknowledgments

Big thanks to Jon Corippo and Marlena Hebern, whose Edu-Protocols have not just changed how I teach but have fundamentally altered my career's trajectory for the better. Your work has created ripples of joy and innovation in classrooms far and wide, including mine.

A heartfelt shout-out to Dave Burgess and the team at DBC, Inc., for creating a platform that elevates teacher voices and provides mentorship. Your belief in my message has been incredibly empowering.

Nathan Collins, my teacher-bestie, deserves special recognition for his unwavering support and partnership through this journey. Your encouragement and insights have been invaluable.

To the countless mentors and colleagues who've shared their wisdom with me, thank you. Your influence has been a critical component of my growth as an educator.

To all the thousands of educators who have shared this journey with me, both in digital and physical spaces, your engagement, feedback, and shared experiences have been a source of constant inspiration and growth.

A big thank you to Kim Voge and the EduProtocols team for your collaboration, friendship, support, and shared vision. The EduProtocols community has been a vibrant hub for this work, fostering connections and growth among educators.

And to my family—Julie, Aiden, Eliza, Zane—your love and support are my foundation. You make all the hard work worth it.

Thank you for being part of this journey.

About Jacob Carr

J acob Carr, known to his friends as Jake, combines his expertise as an educator, author, and consultant to specialize in innovative teaching strategies, including EduProtocols, pedagogy, educational technology, and artificial intelligence. Balancing his professional life with family, Jacob, a father of three, cherishes moments spent paddleboarding, sitting around the firepit, or painting watercolor scenes of nature.

With extensive experience in K-12 education, he has served as a teacher, program administrator, and consultant in both traditional and alternative educational settings. He has delivered keynotes, trainings, and workshops to educators across the United States and internationally. His qualifications include an M.A. in Education, California teaching credentials, and Waldorf certification.

Jacob also co-hosts the "What Teachers Have to Say" podcast with Nathan Collins. This podcast brings together innovative educators to discuss the emotional complexities of teaching, covering topics like access and equity, artificial intelligence, student behavior, teacher burnout, and mentorship models. Listeners can expect practical teaching advice and resources presented in an approachable and real way, along with valuable insights and inspiration for educators at all levels.

In addition to the podcast, and being active on social media, Jacob offers workshops, conference keynotes and presentations, and consulting services. His goal is to support educators in modernizing their teaching practices and enhancing student learning experiences.

More from

Since 2012, DBCI has published books that inspire and equip educators to be their best. For more information on our titles or to purchase bulk orders for your school, district, or book study, visit DaveBurgessConsulting.com/DBCIbooks.

The *Like a PIRATE*™ Series

Teach Like a PIRATE by Dave Burgess

eXPlore Like a PIRATE by Michael Matera

Learn Like a PIRATE by Paul Solarz

Plan Like a PIRATE by Dawn M. Harris

Play Like a PIRATE by Quinn Rollins

Run Like a PIRATE by Adam Welcome

Tech Like a PIRATE by Matt Miller

The *Lead Like a PIRATE*™ Series

Lead Like a PIRATE by Shelley Burgess and Beth Houf

Balance Like a PIRATE by Jessica Cabeen, Jessica Johnson, and Sarah Johnson

Lead beyond Your Title by Nili Bartley

Lead with Appreciation by Amber Teamann and Melinda Miller

Lead with Collaboration by Allyson Apsey and Jessica Gomez

Lead with Culture by Jay Billy

Lead with Instructional Rounds by Vicki Wilson

Lead with Literacy by Mandy Ellis

She Leads by Dr. Rachael George and Majalise W. Tolan

The *EduProtocol Field Guide* Series

Deploying EduProtocols by Kim Voge, with Jon Corippo and Marlena Hebern

The EduProtocol Field Guide by Marlena Hebern and Jon Corippo

The EduProtocol Field Guide: Book 2 by Marlena Hebern and Jon Corippo

The EduProtocol Field Guide: Math Edition by Lisa Nowakowski and Jeremiah Ruesch

The EduProtocol Field Guide: Primary Edition by Benjamin Cogswell and Jennifer Dean

The EduProtocol Field Guide: Social Studies Edition by Dr. Scott M. Petri and Adam Moler

Leadership & School Culture

Beyond the Surface of Restorative Practices by Marisol Rerucha

Change the Narrative by Henry J. Turner and Kathy Lopes

Choosing to See by Pamela Seda and Kyndall Brown

Culturize by Jimmy Casas

Discipline Win by Andy Jacks

Educate Me! by Dr. Shree Walker with Micheal D. Ison

Escaping the School Leader's Dunk Tank by Rebecca Coda and Rick Jetter

Fight Song by Kim Bearden

From Teacher to Leader by Starr Sackstein

If the Dance Floor Is Empty, Change the Song by Joe Clark

The Innovator's Mindset by George Couros

It's OK to Say "They" by Christy Whittlesey

Kids Deserve It! by Todd Nesloney and Adam Welcome

Leading the Whole Teacher by Allyson Apsey

Let Them Speak by Rebecca Coda and Rick Jetter

The Limitless School by Abe Hege and Adam Dovico

Live Your Excellence by Jimmy Casas

Next-Level Teaching by Jonathan Alsheimer

The Pepper Effect by Sean Gaillard

Principaled by Kate Barker, Kourtney Ferrua, and Rachael George

The Principled Principal by Jeffrey Zoul and Anthony McConnell

Relentless by Hamish Brewer

The Secret Solution by Todd Whitaker, Sam Miller, and Ryan Donlan

Start. Right. Now. by Todd Whitaker, Jeffrey Zoul, and Jimmy Casas

Stop. Right. Now. by Jimmy Casas and Jeffrey Zoul

Teach Your Class Off by CJ Reynolds

Teachers Deserve It by Rae Hughart and Adam Welcome

They Call Me "Mr. De" by Frank DeAngelis

Thrive through the Five by Jill M. Siler

Unmapped Potential by Julie Hasson and Missy Lennard

When Kids Lead by Todd Nesloney and Adam Dovico

Word Shift by Joy Kirr

Your School Rocks by Ryan McLane and Eric Lowe

Technology & Tools

50 Things to Go Further with Google Classroom by Alice Keeler and Libbi Miller

50 Things You Can Do with Google Classroom by Alice Keeler and Libbi Miller

50 Ways to Engage Students with Google Apps by Alice Keeler and Heather Lyon

140 Twitter Tips for Educators by Brad Currie, Billy Krakower, and Scott Rocco

Block Breaker by Brian Aspinall

Building Blocks for Tiny Techies by Jamila "Mia" Leonard

Code Breaker by Brian Aspinall

The Complete EdTech Coach by Katherine Goyette and Adam Juarez

Control Alt Achieve by Eric Curts

The Esports Education Playbook by Chris Aviles, Steve Isaacs, Christine Lion-Bailey, and Jesse Lubinsky

Google Apps for Littles by Christine Pinto and Alice Keeler

Master the Media by Julie Smith

Raising Digital Leaders by Jennifer Casa-Todd

Reality Bytes by Christine Lion-Bailey, Jesse Lubinsky, and Micah Shippee, PhD

Sail the 7 Cs with Microsoft Education by Becky Keene and Kathi Kersznowski

Shake Up Learning by Kasey Bell

Social LEADia by Jennifer Casa-Todd

Stepping Up to Google Classroom by Alice Keeler and Kimberly Mattina

Teaching Math with Google Apps by Alice Keeler and Diana Herrington

Teaching with Google Jamboard by Alice Keeler and Kimberly Mattina

Teachingland by Amanda Fox and Mary Ellen Weeks

Teaching Methods & Materials

All 4s and 5s by Andrew Sharos

Boredom Busters by Katie Powell

The Classroom Chef by John Stevens and Matt Vaudrey

The Collaborative Classroom by Trevor Muir

Copyrighteous by Diana Gill

CREATE by Bethany J. Petty

Ditch That Homework by Matt Miller and Alice Keeler

Ditch That Textbook by Matt Miller

Don't Ditch That Tech by Matt Miller, Nate Ridgway, and Angelia Ridgway

EDrenaline Rush by John Meehan

Educated by Design by Michael Cohen, The Tech Rabbi

Empowered to Choose: A Practical Guide to Personalized Learning by Andrew Easton

Expedition Science by Becky Schnekser

Frustration Busters by Katie Powell

Fully Engaged by Michael Matera and John Meehan

Game On? Brain On! by Lindsay Portnoy, PhD

Guided Math AMPED by Reagan Tunstall

Happy & Resilient by Roni Habib

Innovating Play by Jessica LaBar-Twomy and Christine Pinto

Instant Relevance by Denis Sheeran

Instructional Coaching Connection by Nathan Lang-Raad

Keeping the Wonder by Jenna Copper, Ashley Bible, Abby Gross, and Staci Lamb

LAUNCH by John Spencer and A.J. Juliani

Learning in the Zone by Dr. Sonny Magana

Lights, Cameras, TEACH! by Kevin J. Butler

Make Learning MAGICAL by Tisha Richmond

Pass the Baton by Kathryn Finch and Theresa Hoover

Project-Based Learning Anywhere by Lori Elliott

Pure Genius by Don Wettrick

The Revolution by Darren Ellwein and Derek McCoy

The Science Box by Kim Adsit and Adam Peterson

Shift This! by Joy Kirr

Skyrocket Your Teacher Coaching by Michael Cary Sonbert

Spark Learning by Ramsey Musallam

Sparks in the Dark by Travis Crowder and Todd Nesloney

Table Talk Math by John Stevens

Teachables by Cheryl Abla and Lisa Maxfield

Unpack Your Impact by Naomi O'Brien and LaNesha Tabb

The Wild Card by Hope and Wade King

Writefully Empowered by Jacob Chastain

The Writing on the Classroom Wall by Steve Wyborney

You Are Poetry by Mike Johnston

You'll Never Guess What I'm Saying by Naomi O'Brien

You'll Never Guess What I'm Thinking About by Naomi O'Brien

Inspiration, Professional Growth & Personal Development

Be REAL by Tara Martin

Be the One for Kids by Ryan Sheehy

The Coach ADVenture by Amy Illingworth

Creatively Productive by Lisa Johnson

The Ed Branding Book by Dr. Renae Bryant and Lynette White

Educational Eye Exam by Alicia Ray

The EduNinja Mindset by Jennifer Burdis

Empower Our Girls by Lynmara Colón and Adam Welcome

Finding Lifelines by Andrew Grieve and Andrew Sharos

The Four O'Clock Faculty by Rich Czyz

How Much Water Do We Have? by Pete and Kris Nunweiler

P Is for Pirate by Dave and Shelley Burgess

A Passion for Kindness by Tamara Letter

The Path to Serendipity by Allyson Apsey

PheMOMenal Teacher by Annick Rauch

Recipes for Resilience by Robert A. Martinez

Rogue Leader by Rich Czyz

Sanctuaries by Dan Tricarico

Saving Sycamore by Molly B. Hudgens

The Secret Sauce by Rich Czyz

Shattering the Perfect Teacher Myth by Aaron Hogan

Stories from Webb by Todd Nesloney

Talk to Me by Kim Bearden

Teach Better by Chad Ostrowski, Tiffany Ott, Rae Hughart, and Jeff Gargas

Teach Me, Teacher by Jacob Chastain

Teach, Play, Learn! by Adam Peterson

The Teachers of Oz by Herbie Raad and Nathan Lang-Raad

TeamMakers by Laura Robb and Evan Robb

Through the Lens of Serendipity by Allyson Apsey

Write Here and Now by Dan Tricarico

The Zen Teacher by Dan Tricarico

Children's Books

The Adventures of Little Mickey by Mickey Smith Jr.

Alpert by LaNesha Tabb

Alpert & Friends by LaNesha Tabb

Beyond Us by Aaron Polansky

Cannonball In by Tara Martin

Dolphins in Trees by Aaron Polansky

Dragon Smart by Tisha and Tommy Richmond

I Can Achieve Anything by MoNique Waters

I Want to Be a Lot by Ashley Savage

The Magic of Wonder by Jenna Copper, Ashley Bible, Abby Gross, and Staci Lamb

Micah's Big Question by Naomi O'Brien

The Princes of Serendip by Allyson Apsey

Ride with Emilio by Richard Nares

A Teacher's Top Secret Confidential by LaNesha Tabb

A Teacher's Top Secret: Mission Accomplished by LaNesha Tabb

The Wild Card Kids by Hope and Wade King

Zom-Be a Design Thinker by Amanda Fox

Made in the USA
Columbia, SC
19 October 2024

44724831R10107